An Illustrated Histo
of

OLDHAM'S
RAILWAYS

by

John Hooper

ACKNOWLEDGEMENTS.

I would like to thank first of all the photographers, who so kindly allowed me access to their collections, for without their hospitality, kindness and patience this album could not have been compiled with such a varied selection; Jim Cocker, Jim Davenport, Richard S.Greenwood, Brian Hilton, Ian Holt, and Peter Hutchinson come to mind. Their enthusiasm for the project was a joy. Others who supplied material include Roy Anderson, Alex Appleton, Eddie Johnson, J.J.Smith and John Stretton. The Oldham Evening Chronicle gave me access to their files and came up with a couple of gems which were hard to resist. The staff of the Oldham Local Interest Centre were both helpful and efficient when they received my requests to supply documents and photographic material. Former Oldham railwaymen interviewed at length, for those anecdotes and vital snippets of information, include Walter Ackroyd, Rowland Barrett, Jim Davenport, and Eddie Fairgray; all were associated with Lees engine shed and local train workings. Some of the above mentioned were further pestered to read the proofs and I should like to include amongst the 'readers', Chris Hawkins and George Reeve. Organisations who have kindly given assistance include BR London Midland Region, Greater Manchester County Record Office, the National Railway Museum, York, Oldham Libraries and the Public Record Office, Kew. To you all many thanks.

IRWELL
PRESS

Copyright Irwell Press 1991.

ISBN 871608 19 8.

*First published in the United Kingdom 1991 by
IRWELL PRESS.
3 Durley Avenue, Pinner, Middlesex, HA5 1JQ.*

Printed by Amadeus Press, Huddersfield.

Set at the edge of the steep western slopes of the Pennines and overlooking the Lancashire Plain from its lofty perch on top of a 600ft hill, the town of Oldham with its surrounding districts was chosen, more by nature than man, as home to the greatest cotton spinning industry the world had ever seen. The damp climate was ideal for spinning the fragile fibres into workable textiles for growing home and world markets. These conditions were not, it may be added, ideal for the people who worked within the industry. But cotton brought jobs and (for some) prosperity; the Industrial Revolution was a fact, the population of Britain was booming and Oldham wanted some of the wealth on offer.

To become part of the burgeoning industrial power of Britain in the 1830s, it was necessary to have good transport (very much after the fashion of today's motorway networks) – canals, turnpikes and the newly invented though very promising railway. The geographical location of Oldham did not offer a very easy route for canals (perhaps if the railway had not been invented canals would have one day reached the town centre) and history shows that it was by–passed by two of the more important canals of the day, the Rochdale and the Huddersfield Narrow. Railways did however offer a solution, in their infancy, that was to prove successful, rewarding and vital for Oldham.

The Act authorising the building of the first railway to Oldham was given Royal Assent on the 1st July 1839 (just four days before the Manchester & Leeds Railway opened from Manchester Oldham Road to Littleborough). Late the following year, a route was surveyed which was to bring a line from a point on the Manchester & Leeds Railway near Middleton, elevation 342 feet, to a terminus on the western side of Oldham at Werneth, elevation 528 feet. Within its mere two miles, the Oldham branch was to rise nearly two hundred feet; included in the plan was an incline with an elevation of 1 foot in every 27 travelled, which was to be the steepest locomotive worked passenger gradient in Britain. Accounting for nearly half the total length of the new railway, the Werneth Incline, as it became known, was to be worked by two locomotives attached to a wire rope, which passed over a 17 foot diameter wheel sited at the top (Werneth end) of the

ferocious gradient. Secured at the other end of the wire rope were ballast wagons to retard the forces of gravity.

The line opened on the 31st March 1842 and the incline section was worked from the outset by wire rope. I do not intend to go into any detail as to the workings of the incline as these have been adequately covered in other publications and technical papers, suffice to say that the 'rope method' was used for a further ten years before passenger trains were entrusted wholly to locomotive power. Goods trains though, if heavy, were to use 'the rope' until about 1854, when such haulage ceased completely.

The branch line to Oldham was a success from its opening and three quarters of a million passengers used it each year during the 1840s. Where the branch joined the Manchester to Leeds railway a station, named appropriately Oldham Junction, was erected and opened on the same day as the branch. By mid August it had been renamed Middleton and some ten years later it became Middleton Junction.

Werneth terminus in the meantime was found to be too far away from Oldham town centre for convenience and so plans to extend the railway to Mumps were drawn up in 1844. The high ground immediately to the east of Werneth presented the first obstacle (it was this that had prevented the initial branch line from reaching the centre of town from the outset) and two tunnels, Werneth at 471 yards and Central at 449 yards, rising on a gradient of 1 in 80, had to be driven through the hill. An Act dated 30th June 1845 for the extension of the Oldham Branch to Mumps enabled work on the tunnels to be started in the autumn of that year with completion less than two years later on the 6th August 1847. In the previous month the Lancashire & Yorkshire Railway was born from the amalgamation of the Manchester & Leeds and its Oldham Branch and other railways (see Marshall *The Lancashire & Yorkshire Railway* D&C 1970) and so an early form of the L&Y crest was incorporated into the stonework surrounding the western end of Werneth tunnel. The extension to Mumps with an intermediate station named Central was completed in late October and the line was opened to passenger traffic on the 1st November 1847. The first stage of Oldham's railway development was now complete. All that remained for the

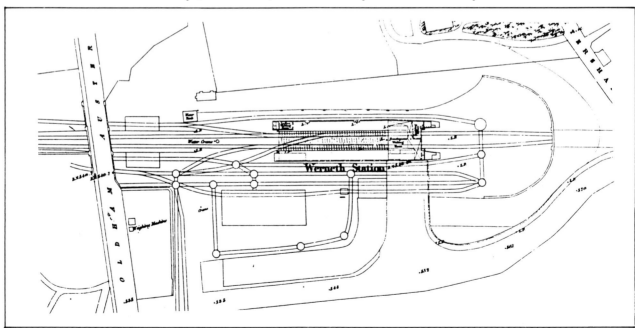

Werneth station and environs in 1848. The overall roof, as can be seen, extended the full length of the existing platforms. Goods facilities were concentrated on the south side of the station with numerous wagon turntables serving the sidings and goods sheds. The lines leading off across what was to become Railway Road, continued a few hundred yards further to a coal wharf. On the north side of the site a single line of track leads under the road bridge into the Hartford Iron Works of Messrs Platt Brothers. Either side of the main line, to the right of the road bridge, two single road sheds stand opposite each other; either or both could have been used to house locomotives, stabling overnight in Oldham, although one was probably a coking shed for refuelling the motive power of the period. On the right, the by now completed Werneth tunnel is depicted by two dotted lines.

Western portal of Werneth tunnel, 30th March 1968, with the early form of L&YR crest still adorning the capping stones.

A. J. Cocker.

L&YR in Oldham for the time being was consolidation, before competition reared its ugly head.

A branch to Oldham from the Manchester–Huddersfield line at Greenfield was opened by the London & North Western Railway on the 4th July 1856, with passenger services starting the following day. The terminus in Oldham was a temporary affair named Victoria Station and was adjacent to the L&Y's Mumps station. A junction was made with the L&Y and a one road engine shed was erected for the engine that would work the branch, with a turntable completing the facilities. The LNWR branch was quite a formidable engineering undertaking with cuttings, bridges and the Lydgate tunnel, just over three quarters of a mile long, between Grotton and Grasscroft. A Board of Trade report dated 12th June 1856 stated: *I have the honour to report etc. 11th June 1856, I have this day inspected the Oldham branch of the L&NW Railway. This branch, which is a double line, is a little less than 4 miles in length, extends between Mumps and Greenfield, connecting the L&Y and the Manchester and Huddersfield Railway and forming a communication from the latter to the town of Oldham. It is not proposed however to work the passenger traffic further than the L&NW Oldham Station. The permanent way is laid in a substantial manner, with rails from 18 to 21 feet in length, and weighing 80lbs to the linear yard connected by fish joints and supported in cast iron chairs upon transverse sleepers, 2ft apart at the points and 3ft 2ins from centre to centre elsewhere. The works are heavy containing a tunnel 1332 yards long through the coal formation. The gradients are severe and the curves sharp. The bridges are 19 in number 9 over and 10 under the railway. The spans of the former vary from 26 to 61 feet, and those of the latter from 6 to 44 ft. Two of the former are 27ft and 38ft spans and two of the latter, of 12 and 15 ft spans are constructed of cast iron girders on masonry abutments, and the remainder are composed entirely of brickwork and masonry. All these works appear to be substantially constructed; and I am of the opinion that this line may be opened without danger to the public using the same.*

The Oldham, Ashton & Guide Bridge Railway entered the town from the south, on a line from Ashton, in August 1861; built under an Act of 1857 it was operated jointly by the L&NWR and the Manchester, Sheffield & Lincolnshire Railway (later becoming the Great Central). In June 1862, the two companies absorbed the railway under a joint leasing arrangement and from thereon it went under the somewhat unwieldly title, OA&GB Joint, each partner eventually holding 150,000 shares with a further 40,000 being issued to the public. The Oldham station for the OA&GB was sited at Clegg Street, virtually next door to the Lancashire & Yorkshire's Central station, with the line forming a junction to that railway slightly to the east of the two. Only one intermediate station was erected on the OA&GB route to Ashton, at Park Bridge. The following Board of Trade notes are of interest.....
An Agreement dated 1860 between the Manchester Sheffield and Lincolnshire Railway hereinafter called The Manchester Company and the Oldham Ashton Under Lyne and Guide Bridge Junction Company afterwards called the Oldham Company... By an Act of Parliament passed in the 21st year of the reign of her present majesty Queen Victoria an Act for the

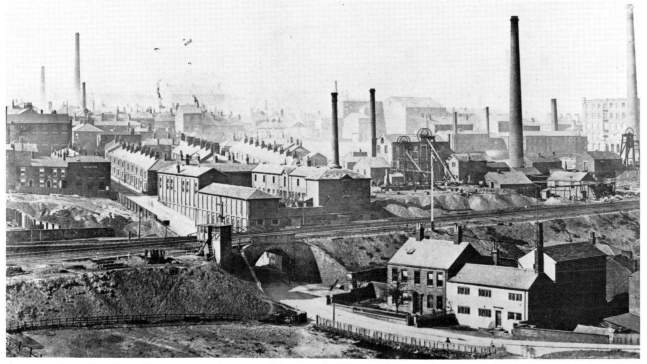

In an easterly continuation of the rear cover view, we find the extended Waterloo Street bridge now carrying the tracks of the OA&GB as well as those of the original occupant, the L&YR. Over the next twenty–odd years the houses in the foreground were to disappear and the depressed land facing was to be infilled for expanding railway facilities. The signalbox, with signals sticking out through the hipped roof, is one of the original OA&GB boxes extended from its earlier form. Rhodes Bank colliery chimney dominates this area of town.

Looking now towards Mumps, in the same year as the previous view, we can just make out, from left to right, a very busy Stoneyard sidings, Oldham Junction signalbox and then the original, two–platformed, L&YR Mumps station complete with footbridge; this footbridge was not part of the earlier station scheme and was built only when the line was extended to Rochdale. The overhead crane of Mumps goods yard stands on a timber gantry which was to be replaced some years later by a steel girder affair (see page 52). In front of that we have the single road engine shed of the L&NWR with its roof mounted smoke ventilators sticking up to give some idea of its length. There are cotton mills, large and small, everywhere. The town was expanding with the cotton industry and the railway was doing likewise. The British Empire was still in the making.

construction of railways to supply direct communication between Oldham, Ashton Under Lyne and Guide Bridge, and for the accommodation of the Neighbourhood.... The Oldham Railway is now in course of construction and nearly complete.

The Agreement is for the use of, and working by the Manchester Company of all or any part of the railway.....and the use of the works and conveniences belonging thereto. The Oldham Company to complete all works.....including such stations, wharfs, offices, sheds, warehouses, repairing shops, sidings, watering places, water supply, coal drops, repairing machinery, apparatus and other works in connection therewith.

When opened and everything was in working order the Manchester Company *shall with their engines carriages vans and other vehicles use and work all and every Part of the said Oldham Railway and for that purpose shall have the full free and uninterrupted use and passage with their engines carriages wagons vans etc. over and along the Oldham Company's line of railway and every part thereof. The Manchester Company shall find and provide all working and rolling stock required at their own cost....the Manchester Company shall have the entire management of the railway....etc etc....the Oldham Company shall have the right to inspect the line from time to time and repairs etc. shall be carried out by the Manchester Company. The Manchester Company shall provide and employ on and about the line all such station masters, agents, booking clerk, porters and other officers workmen and servants as shall be proper and efficient for the due working of the line.*

Subsequently the LNWR (this would be during 1860) objected to the Agreement; there is no proper conclusion in Board of Trade notes dated 5th January 1861, these simply agree to pass on the objections....

The Bill of 10th August 1857 stated that the railway was...*to afford direct communication between the towns of Oldham Ashton under Lyne Stalybridge and Guide Bridge in the County Palatine of Lancaster with branches therefrom to places in the Neighbourhood... proposed railway will! communicate with railways of the Manchester Sheffield and Lincolnshire Company — its name shall be the Oldham Ashton Under Lyne and Guide Bridge Junction Railway...* there were to be 14,000 shares at £10 each. Some sample tolls were:–

Class 1 – with respect to the conveyance of goods including Lime, limestone, salt, dung, compost and all sorts of manure and all undressed material for the repairs of highways, coal, slack, cannel, coke, culm and cinders a penny per ton per mile.

Class 2 – one penny halfpenny per ton per mile – building stone, bricks, tiles, slate, clay, sand, chalk, marl, iron, ironstone and iron–ore, copper, tin, lead, pig iron, bar iron, rod iron, hoop iron, sheet iron and all similar descriptions of wrought iron etc etc. Class 3 – 2d per ton per mile – sugar, grain, corn, flour, hides, dyewoods, Manchester packs, earthenware, timber staves and deals, metals except iron etc.

Class 4 – 3d per mile all cotton and other wools, drugs manufactured goods, merchandise, fish etc. articles matters or Things.

Inspection by the Board of Trade was on 12th July 1861: *I have this day inspected the Oldham Ashton Under Lyne and Guide Bridge Junction Railways from the Junction at Guide Bridge to Oldham. A portion of this line from the junction at Guide Bridge with the main line of the Manchester Sheffield & Lincolnshire Railway to a junction with the Stalybridge branch of the Lancashire and Yorkshire Railway near Ashton Under Lyne was formally inspected by the Board and the opening postponed. The notice of opening was subsequently withdrawn and I have now been supplied with the details of the line from another junction with the Stalybridge branch of the Lancashire and Yorkshire Railway near Ashton to a junction with the Oldham branch of the London North Western, a length of 4 miles 2½ chains. The line is double throughout* ...The most notable engineering feature was 'the important viaduct' 12 arches of 50 ft span built in stone 'nearly 100 ft high, and a 55 yard tunnel' The inspector declined to recommend opening through the incompleteness of the work; the signalling was found to be wrong ('too many levers'),– stations were on the wrong gradient, – over–bridges not strong enough to carry a locomotive and so on. *Portions of the line are incomplete. There are symptoms of subsidence in the masonry of the Park Bridge Viaduct at the south end and to a lesser extent some of the piers at the other end....* So the OA&GB did not get off to a good start but certain of the above problems must have been put right virtually straight away – such as signalling – for the railway opened for business the following month. In 1868 the OA&GB carried 515,937 passengers bringing in revenue of £8,356, freight carried amounted to 61,800 tons earning just under £3,000. By 1921 the passenger figures were down to 360,277 which included 129 season ticket holders; freight figures were even more disastrous – just 6,760 tons and 8 head of cattle, a bad year indeed.

The next railway development took place in 1863 when the L&YR opened its line from Mumps, by way of Shaw & Crompton and Milnrow, to Rochdale where it connected with the main line to Leeds. This line formed a somewhat circuitous though easier route to Manchester and took two years to complete, costing in the process over £350,000. Earthwork amounting to 177,000 cubic yards had to be excavated on the section between Mumps and Jubilee bridge at Shaw, much of it around Higginshaw where the high ground made cuttings necessary. The Board of Trade Report of 27th October 1863 declares....*I have this day inspected the Oldham and Rochdale branch of the Lancashire and Yorkshire Railway. The works reported in my letters of 11th and 12th of August have been altered and are now satisfactory except for the under bridge girders....*Whatever the Inspector's objections to certain girders it was obviously corrected or explained away by the L&Y for the following day he further reported.....*no longer object to the line in question etc.....* The branch to Royton was also contracted but this was not completed until 21st March 1864. Stations were erected at Shaw, Newhey and Milnrow, ready for the opening of the Rochdale line to passengers in early November. Goods trains had however been using the line since mid–August giving some relief to the heavily worked Werneth incline. Royton Junction station only opened four months after the Royton branch came into operation.

Excepting the Hollinwood railway, which was a later enterprise, the lines around Oldham were now all in place and consolidation and expansion was to proceed over the next forty years, the 1880s especially being a time of prosperity and growth. Manchester was to become the cotton capital of the world but only in name; dubbed in the contemporary press *Cottonopolis*, Oldham with its satellite townships was the cotton spinning *capital*, having nearly a third of the total spinning capacity of the United Kingdom. Cotton was therefore to play a great role in the running of the local railways – raw cotton in and finished products out – transporting and storing the vast quantities needed became a speciality with which only the railway companies could cope. Huge, purpose built warehouses became commonplace as did the large coal yards catering for domestic as well as industrial needs.

Oldham never was served by any main line railway, most probably because of the town's geographical location; railway companies always sought the easiest route for their main lines. There was never a huge main station with a great arched roof, like Manchester Central or York, even though the population was nearly three times larger than the latter place. A report, brought about after a survey of the town's transport in 1948, recommended that a single large station be built on the site of Central and Clegg Street, with a nearby bus interchange, easy access to the proposed inner ring road and pedestrian walkways from the town centre. Alas the scheme never came about; perhaps the superb public road transport system in South–East Lancashire kept local railway passenger levels below the cost threshold for such a scheme and succesive postwar governments have never been generous to the nationalised railway. But it wasn't passengers that kept the Oldham railways alive even then, despite the hordes that took their annual holidays at the seaside during the Wakes.

King Cotton and the railways grew together and the same can be said about their eventual decline. In 1929 some 58% of the insured workers in Oldham worked within the cotton industry, by 1948 that was down to 29% and today the percentage is in single figures, falling ever more each month. When the cotton industry slowly bled to death after World War Two then so did the railway that served it.

Only one line now remains open through the town, serving stations at Hollinwood, Werneth, Mumps, Derker and Shaw, from where it is singled to Rochdale. The future of even that line is continually in the balance, financial support from the Greater Manchester Passenger Transport Authority ensuring a life that is reviewed annually. Perhaps if Oldham had been on a major cross–Pennine route things might have been different, at least as far as passenger services go. What is certain is that the industry for which Oldham became famous is gone forever and with it the freight trains. A railway can only be wholly self supportive with freight revenue and so what chance does the Oldham line have without freight traffic? The future looks grim indeed but, let's put doubt aside for the time being and look at what was once the great little railway system of the town on the top of a hill, twixt mill and moor.

A JOURNEY AROUND THE SYSTEM.

To explain the railway system around the area we will journey along the various lines radiating from central Oldham, using Gas Street footbridge (a long lattice girder affair straddling a central position between Mumps and the erstwhile Central and Clegg Street stations) as the starting point for each journey, and a description of each route taken will be given as it would have been in about 1950.

To Chadderton Goods junction via the Werneth incline and including the Hollinwood line.

On a falling gradient we first notice on our right the Oldham Corporation refuse destructor, a sinister range of buildings topped with a huge chimney, then the gas works with sidings alongside used for stabling coaching stock. Mumps No.1 signalbox sees us safely over the junction from the OA&GB to our left. Approaching Central station the gradient falls even more and to the left we glimpse Clegg Street station just before we go under the road bridge and into the cutting containing Central station itself. Through Central and the cutting gets deeper as we plunge into the 449 yards of Central tunnel, the line curving to the right as we thread the darkness, suddenly bursting into sunlight (well the light anyway) for a few seconds as the train gathers speed at the bottom of this, the deepest cutting in Oldham. Back into darkness the train slows in the gloom of Werneth tunnel (471 yards) ready for the stop at Werneth station. Into the daylight for a moment we enter the dreariness of the station with its overline booking hall but just before that on the right, next to the tunnel mouth is a small signalbox Werneth No.2 and behind that the ex 'Lanky' 'Continuous Pilot' coalstage still in use. One of Newton Heath's 0–6–0 saddletanks simmers away beside it, the crew taking on some coal; this shunting engine works the mineral and goods yards behind the station that stretch down to Middleton Road some distance away to the north. Behind the station to the left is another small goods yard, the first such yard in Oldham and it too has a shed albeit a small one due to the space restrictions of the site. On leaving, on the level, we immediately start the descent of the 1 in 27 Werneth Incline, and to our left the Hollinwood branch

Stock Lane bridge, Chadderton, on the Werneth Incline.

A. J. Cocker.

descends too, towards Manchester by the later and more direct route to 'Cottonopolis'. Under the Featherstall Road bridge the New Hartford works of Messrs Platt Brothers looms on the right; connections off the main line lead into an extensive internal rail system, on such a scale that Platts employ a dozen steam locomotives of their own, as well as a large wagon fleet. Not all of the locomotives are used within this particular site a few being stationed at the East Works near Mumps. Continuing down the incline we are now on an embankment passing over Lansdowne Road and on either side the view is filled with dozens of cotton mills, their chimneys spewing out clouds of smoke as the industry grasps onto the few remaining years of proceeding decline. At Stock Lane bridge the gradient eases slightly, only 1 in 30 now! On the left, the site of the long-defunct Stockfield colliery and beyond that the green fields of Chadderton, next comes Broadway bridge where the line is in a slight cutting for a few hundred yards. The worst of the incline is now behind us and the brakes can be eased off somewhat as the line levels out. With speed picking up we round a gentle curve and see, on the right, the junction of the goods only branch line coming in from Chadderton coal yard; opened in August 1914 the branch was built to serve the numerous large cotton mills springing up in the Chadderton district, as King Cotton strengthened his economic hold on the area. At this point we finish our journey on the Middleton Junction to Oldham branch of the former Lancashire & Yorkshire Railway and return to Werneth station for a trip to Hollinwood.

Curving to the left from the incline branch we now join the newer of the L&Y routes to Manchester. Noticeable straight away is the alarming descent of the Werneth Incline as it drops away to our right and already, with less than a hundred yards travelled, the line must be twenty or so feet below. Our train lurches to the left as we traverse a high embankment over the rooftops, row upon row of terraced housing; over Suthers Street, Edward Street and Block Lane in no time as we accelerate ever faster down the hill. You want the train to slow so that you can take in more of what is passing; industrial and grimy it may be but fascinating from this superb vantage point. Over Wash Brook and with not much of railway interest to grab our attention at the moment you can look to the west and see Manchester and Salford in the distance, both cities straddled with the ever present gloom of industrial haze. The train starts to slow now and as we round the curve near Rose Mill, Hollinwood comes into view. Over Drury Lane bridge and to the left is the goods yard with its two warehouses; the first one that we pass towered over its older neighbour and was opened in December 1885 at a cost of £20,873 14/1d. The 'older neighbour' was completed in January 1882 having cost £3,534 8/6d and from the time scale between the completion of both buildings and their relative costs (inflation was virtually zero then) it can be appreciated, perhaps, just how much impact the new railway had on the commerce of the township. Into Hollinwood station now, its platforms straddling Bower Lane on a low bridge that has become

infamous to local road transport concerns. On the Up platform stands the signalbox, not one of the lofty type usually found but instead a medium length, squat wooden structure that enabled the platform dweller, especially the enthusiast, to observe the signalman as he went about his business. Just west of the station and on either side of the line are the premises of Ferranti Electrical Engineering; both works are rail served, with a single track on the Up side usually occupied by a huge Well-wagon used for transporting the transformers made here. The sidings on the Down side have a group of six tracks, used by the still-thriving local coal merchants. The works on this side of the line are the newer of the pair and were built on the site of another long-defunct mine, known as Bower colliery. Here our journey on Oldham's youngest railway line ends and we return back up the hill to Gas Street footbridge.

To Jubilee via Royton Junction and the branch to Royton.

Staying on the old Lanky route but now heading east we parallel the OA&GB for a few hundred yards on its way to Glodwick Road station. To our left is the site of the one time Rhodes Bank colliery, yet another owned by the Chamber Coll. Co. Mumps No.2 signalbox is followed by Stoneyard sidings, so named because there was, up to the end of the last century, a large yard here processing all manner of finished stone for both domestic and industrial use. There was also once a small goods warehouse, erected in the 1840s to serve the newly arrived L&YR. Entering Mumps station now, the line starts to curve to the north, the screeching of wheel flanges giving some indication of the change in direction. Prior to 1884 Mumps had two platforms, separated by the Up and Down lines, and joined by a footbridge. However widening, enlargement and re-arrangement, costing in excess of £22,000, during the period August 1884 to late 1887 saw the now familiar island platform take shape, with its central facilities and single line bays at each end. The original station dated from 1847. With wheel flanges still complaining we continue our journey passing on the right, at platform end, Mumps goods yard with its gantry crane, cattle pens, warehouse and ever-present pilot engine which today is a former Lanky A Class 0-6-0. Mumps No.3 signalbox comes next as we pass over the bridges at Whitehead Street and then Mumps, Wallshaw Street bus depot dominates the view to the left as we head north towards Rochdale. Lofty stone walls block the view now but high ground rises above the railway and we are once again in a cutting before emerging from under Shaw Road bridge. On our immediate right is Hartford or Lower Moor goods yard, a rail connection from this yard crossing Derker Street into the Hartford Old Works of Messrs Platts, designated a level crossing it is ungated but nevertheless controlled by a signal, unusually sited in the street. The sidings at Hartford goods dated from the late 1860s

Hollinwood in October 1958 before the gardeners got busy with their spades.

Authors collection.

but further lines were laid in 1888 at a cost of £2,602 and the huge cotton warehouse beside Cromford Street was brought into use at the same time, its cost, at almost £18,000 nearly ten times that of the original (though smaller) warehouse in the yard. This building was, in 1914, rented out to Platts who continued to use it until it was demolished at some time during the Second War. Completing the arrangements at Hartford were two cranes, a 5 ton example in the yard and a 4 ton, steam powered, travelling crane used in that part of the site given over to timber storage. Just at the head of the yard a signalbox (with 38 levers and 4 spares) named simply 'Hartford Sidings' controlled the main line and various goods loop connections from this and another yard (dating from the 1890s) on the opposite side of the line. This later set of sidings was used mainly to store complete train loads of goods either originating in the area or arriving for distribution. In the summer, carriages would be positioned here ready for the start of Oldham Wakes but the more usual occupants were coal or empty tar wagons. The yard was laid during 1894-95 and the resultant lengthening of Yates Street overbridge at the southern end cost over £5,700 to complete. As we pass the north end of the yard we see another bridge, carrying Holyrood Street, which was lengthened during the widening of the railway here in 1892-94. Once under Holyrood St we traverse the highest point of the railway system in Oldham (613 ft a.o.d.) and enter Royton Junction where the line to Royton diverges to the left by the signalbox. As we pass through the station there are fans of sidings on either side, no less than thirteen in each group and varying in length from 500 to 700 feet. There are no goods facilities here, only the sorting and storage of wagons. Continuing on towards Shaw & Crompton we have on our left, at the northern end of Royton Junction sidings, another rail served private concern in the shape of Woodstock Mill. Into open country now the line is on a falling gradient of 1 in 260, passing under the hump backed bridge at Bullcote Lane and following the course of the River Beal, along the boundary of Oldham County Borough and the Urban District of Shaw & Crompton. Sholver Moor and Dog Hill, with dairy farms clinging to their slopes, rise to over 1100ft and dominate the view to the right. Easterly, snow laden, winds in the winter cause drifting along this exposed stretch of the line which over the years has seen its quota of blockages. Cotton mills once again come into view as we slow for our entry into Shaw & Crompton. Nearly three dozen large mills are to be found here, the first one we pass on the Up side is Lilac; built during the First World War its neighbouring site to the south was in November 1918 designated to become an aircraft factory – the Board Of Trade was asked on the 11th November 1918 by the L&YR to inspect a new trailing connection from the Up sidings to 'the Government aircraft factory' south of Shaw station! The end of the Great War (on that very day, the 11th November) no doubt ensured that no aircraft industry would arise in Shaw, of all places. Over Beal Lane level crossing we enter Shaw & Crompton station which over the years has been variously named: Shaw, Crompton, Crompton & Shaw and Shaw & Crompton, the changes playing havoc with the railway guides and timetables. Press reports in the 1920s state that Shaw was once reputed to be the richest town in the land with numerous cotton millionaires (barons) living within the district. The boom years of 1919 and 1920 saw work for everyone in the town, and prosperity for the few, however the Depression years of the late 1920s–1930s which affected the whole country also brought its share of misery to Shaw. Leaving the station behind we notice now on our left the large cotton warehouse. Opened by the L&Y in 1888, it is still in business albeit not as briskly as those boom years earlier in the century but nevertheless holding its own. On the opposite side of the line are the remains of a short branch, closed about 1900, that served the Bank House colliery near Grains Road. Also on our right is Shaw North signalbox, with its 15 levers, controlling the entrance to the goods yard and the main line; under Linney Lane bridge we continue to follow the course of the Beal towards Jubilee, the limit of our trip on the Oldham–Rochdale branch. The stone skew bridge, elevating

Milnrow Road over the line, temporarily blocks the view as the line curves first left, then right through the valley, leaving Shaw township behind. A footbridge leading from the aptly named Bridge Street to Wood End maintains a right of way to unlikely named 'Goats'. On the left now is a large wooded hillside but of far more railway interest is the sidings of A. A. Crompton with its tiny signalbox. The railway connection here dates from 1891 but a long drawn–out dispute between Crompton and the L&Y over handling rates nearly saw an early demise for the sidings; by 1902 the Master of the Rolls ruled that A. A. Crompton did not have a case against the L&Y who then continued to charge handling rates as though goods were passing through Shaw goods station. Another third of a mile and we arrive at Jubilee, to encounter the remains of Jubilee colliery on our right. Owned by Messrs Platts, it was rail connected on the 27th January 1889, a signalbox bearing the name Jubilee Colliery having 16 working levers with 4 spare, opening at the same time. We now return to Royton Junction for the short journey down the branch to Royton.

Just about to pass over the unmanned crossing at Jubilee, near to the site of the old Platt's colliery, a Bank Hall (Liverpool) based BR Standard Class 4 4–6–0, No.75046 makes light work of an evening Rochdale – Manchester service on the 4th July 1958.

P. Hutchinson.

Originally single, the branch opened in 1864 and a good description of the line is given by the Board of Trade inspecting officer who looked at the undertaking on the 27th February 1864: *The new line is one mile and 20 chains long, it joins the Oldham and Rochdale branch a short distance north of Oldham station and extends thence to the town of Royton which is the only station on this branch. The permanent way is similar to that laid on the Oldham and Rochdale Railway and is in good order. The line is single throughout except at the junction and at Royton station. Land has been purchased for a double line and the works have been constructed for a double line. There are no public level crossings and there is no turntable at Royton but the company propose to work the line with a tank engine which I submit may be permitted for this short length on the receipt of an undertaking to that effect. There are three masonry overbridges two masonry underbridges and one underbridge having wrought iron girders. These works appear substantially constructed and of sufficient strength....* The inspector, though, was not too happy with some of the signalling arrangements and a few other items of a minor nature so permission to open the branch to the public was declined. The L&YR sorted out all of the problems and on the 12th March the Board of Trade gave its blessing. The branch was eventually doubled in 1885 at a cost of £4,000, the initial earthworks carried out twenty odd years previously keeping the costs down. Travelling on the line in 1950 would find one or two alterations and additions from those early days. On starting out from the Junction station we immediately enter a deep cutting as the track bears to the left, a high stone overbridge carrying Higginshaw Lane towering above the train. Beyond the bridge, on the left, is a branch incline leading to Higginshaw gas works which with its own internal rail system boasts four tank engines to handle the traffic. Not only does coal arrive here by rail but certain by–products such as tar and ammonia go out by rail for industrial use elsewhere. The connection to the gas works opened about 1887. Further on now down the gradient we continue to tread a shallow cutting, as far as Turf Lane overbridge, where the land opens out for a short distance before the line dives under Shaw Road bridge and into Royton terminus. Here the original single platform station serves the town unaltered from opening. Once again the cotton industry is much in evidence; mills back onto the goods yard making expansion of the sidings an impossibility now. Royton's goods facilities certainly grew over the years, even if the passenger side didn't, paralleling the growth of the cotton industry. The huge six storey, steel framed cotton and goods warehouse completed in 1893 at a cost of £21,350 complemented two such buildings of an earlier vintage serving the industry.

To Grasscroft via Lees.

Back at Gas Street we now venture east along the former London & North Western route from Greenfield where the Oldham branch splits from that company's trans–Pennine main line. Before the old LNW proper, it is necessary to traverse about a quarter mile of the OA&GB and, although the goods yard on our right belonged at one time to the LNWR, we are on the metals of 'the Joint'. On the far side of the goods yard is the Greenhill electricity generating station, a decrepit installation soon to be decommisioned and downgraded to a sub–station. At one time there was a one road engine shed near this spot belonging to the LNWR but it outgrew its purpose and closed when a shed was built at Lees. Next comes the same company's large Glodwick Road goods warehouse, the forerunner of which was consumed by fire on the 9th June 1891. The *Oldham Chronicle* of the 10th reported it thus ....*Great Fire in Oldham.... broke out at 7.32 p.m.... such a crowd gathered that passing trains* (on the OA&GB) *had difficulty in using the line....* The original warehouse was barely twelve months old on the day of the outbreak; four floors high and 300ft long by 80ft wide, the cost of the fire including the contents consumed amounted to over £90,000, a vast sum in those days. A fire at the L&YR's new Werneth warehouse just weeks before had caused a similar insurance loss. It was to be November of the following year before the LNWR could once again use the Glodwick Road facility. Passing under a footbridge, connecting the warehouse with Hamilton Street we have on our left some of the older goods buildings dating from the 1850s and bordering onto Hamilton Street. Glodwick Road station has a somewhat open aspect at this end but once past the bay platform the gloom of the cutting becomes apparent. Under the bridge we continue in a deep and narrow stone walled cutting for about a quarter of a mile and then for a similar distance in an earth cutting. Overbridges carry Lees Road and then Clarksfield Street above the line until we ride a high embankment over the valley of Lees Brook. The line is continually curving now, first northerly and then in a more easterly direction to skirt round the town of Lees on the right; under the arched bridge of St John Street the line enters Lees station with its stone flagged platforms and (usually) deserted waiting rooms. Just beyond the platform end, on our left, is the small six road engine shed with its 'saw–toothed' northlight roof, decidedly delapidated with timbers shoring up the front section. Being something of a backwater, Lees shed was one of those places where money was hardly ever spent on modernisation and its amenities were basic. The same can be said about the locomotive allocation, nothing glamorous or exciting about a mixture of ex–Lanky, ex–Wessy and some ex–LMS types that could hardly be described as outstanding but, life at Lees goes on with the enginemen doing what was asked of them. Fitters kept the engines running and the clerks did what was necessary, pulling a few strings on the way to make life easier for all concerned. Nobody made a fuss here, nothing was asked and nothing given. At the end of the shed yard was the border between the Red and White Rose counties for now we are heading into Yorkshire and by a fluke of an age old border dispute Lees is bisected by the county boundary. The large goods shed on the opposite side of the line is actually in Yorkshire but you wouldn't know it. Pressing on now we proceed under the skewed Oldham Road bridge towards Grotton, the line now running level with the land so there are no earthworks to speak of, but just before Grotton & Springhead station there are a couple of rail connections to local mills, Springbank on the right and Livingstone Spinning Co. Nestling quietly at the foot of Lydgate Hill is the station. It has the usual trappings of what might be described as a country station, small goods shed, level crossing, footbridge and platforms that were never overtaxed with waiting passengers. On now towards Lydgate tunnel, with the cutting deepening as we near the tunnel mouth. The first hundred yards of the tunnel are curved slightly to the right but after that it is dead straight and if the engine's exhaust wasn't obscuring the view you could see the pinpoint of light at the other end, over half a mile away. The tunnel has four air shafts along its length, the deepest being about 280 feet from rail to hilltop. Back into the open air a road bridge crowns the top of the cutting which brings us to the wooden–platformed Grasscroft Halt, one of the newer manifestations on the line, dating from 1912. This is the limit of our journey on the LNWR Oldham branch, another quarter mile would bring Greenfield Junction but now we must return to central Oldham for the last of our journeys from Gas Street, this time along the Oldham Ashton & Guide Bridge Junction Railway.

To Park Bridge via the Oldham, Ashton & Guide Bridge.

Sidings fill the land to our left as we border the old Lanky route down towards Clegg Street station. First there are those belonging at one time to the Anglo American Oil Co., then Waterloo Sidings, over Waterloo Street bridge. Past Clegg St signalbox, guarding Waterloo Junction, and then as we follow the gradient down to see rising above and to the left the goods yard – shared at one time by the Great Central and the London & North Western, each having their own warehouses, cranes and sidings. Running through the platforms of Clegg St station the air of neglect is very apparent; never quite living up to its expected role as the 'gateway to the capital' the station has over the years become nothing more than a semi–derelict suburban stopping place. Leaving the depression of Clegg St behind we plunge into a short tunnel where the roads from the bay platforms merge with the through roads. Out of the tunnel and under Park Road bridge, the signalbox to our right carries the name of Sheepwashers Lane – Oldham it seems has more than its fair share of almost Medieval place names. Just further on are Scottfield Sidings laid down by the Great Central railway a few years before World War One in anticipation of increasing goods traffic. On our right the change of scene is dramatic with the expanse of Alexandra Park, with its bowling greens, tennis courts, bandstand, ornate boating lake, large greens and myriad of trees; there are

A Newton Heath Fowler 2–6–2T, No.40015, samples some of the winter delights on offer at Lees in 1957. Standing 600ft above sea level, Lees was prone to get a fair share of the seasonal snows.

J. Davenport.

Oldham Clegg St, August 1957. This view, looking south, shows the neglect that was overtaking the station; it closed less than two years later in May 1959 after the last OA&GB service train. Still visible, on the lampposts and roof supports, is the white paint applied in wartime to assist passengers during the blackout.

B. Hilton.

probably more trees here than in the whole of the rest of Oldham. We pass under a footbridge, the first of three straddling this line as far as Park Bridge, and the gradients now are such that an engine hauling a train towards Ashton can virtually shut off steam and drift along after the initial acceleration from Clegg St platform. After passing the site of Honeywell Lane signalbox we dive under a road bridge of the same name. In front of us the line is dead straight for half a mile or so as it falls at 1 in 86, nice easy going unless you're coming the other way. Through a small cutting, the higher ground is to our right and once out of the cutting a clough called Snipe appears below on the left, part of Cherry Valley. The tiny streams found in the cloughs round about feed the River Medlock and the course of the OA&GBJ was no doubt determined by these cloughs. As the line veers slightly to the right we enter a deeper cutting before the last half mile into Park Bridge. In sight now is the nine arch stone viaduct taking us over the Medlock as it winds its way towards Manchester. Arrival at Park Bridge station concludes our imaginary journeys around the Oldham railway system in a year when most of the railway and its buildings and structures were intact and working. The next fifteen years would see great changes not just in and around Oldham but nationwide and usually, in my non–accountant eyes, for the worse. Oldham missed its chance long ago to be part of the inter–city network and the town is unlikely ever to get that chance again.

Welcome to Oldham. Mumps ticket barrier in April 1953.

Authors Collection.

The following photographic record of Oldham's railways was captured in the main during the period 1950–1970 by local photographers to whom I am deeply indebted. I make some apology for the scarcity of views of the period of the Grouping 1923–1947; those particular photographs do not seem to exist in any number, at least not as far as I know. Oldham was one of those towns rarely visited by enthusiasts, probably because no main line trains with named engines passed through. Its only engine shed, at Lees, was small and housed only goods engines and those passenger locomotives of minor importance in the eyes of enthusiasts. However what I have put together will I hope bring back memories to those who are old enough to remember those 'good ol' days', also I hope it will pass on to the younger generation an impression of what it was really like, not too long ago. It is not intended to cover in this book the history of the Delph branch as its rise and decline have been adequately chronicled in a book The Delph Donkey *and, geographically, it does fall outside the boundaries of the Oldham railway network......*

WERNETH & THE INCLINE.

Werneth in June 1964, from the west end. The 1 in 27 incline is by now disused having closed completely from Chadderton Junction in January the previous year, half the work of the signalman in Werneth signal box going with it. The box itself closed in May 1967, its remaining duties taken over by the new Mumps box. On the right is the line running in from Hollinwood, a formidable incline itself (1 in 50 for much of its length) and because of its curvature was subject, as well, to speed restrictions imposed on trains travelling in the Manchester direction. On the left is the long footbridge connecting the station with Featherstall Road and maintaining a public right–of–way with the overline footbridge at the top of the incline.

T. A. Fletcher.

Up, Manchester bound, platform in March 1968, virtually unchanged from the 1880–1890s alterations except for the addition of electric lighting in place of the 19th century town gas. Passengers were treated to a waiting room in 1884 whereas previous to that date the only waiting room was upstairs, in the booking hall. On the brickwork of the booking hall can be seen evidence of the roof line of the original all over structure where it butted up to the building, the staggered position of the windows gives a further idea of the roof line. New roofs (canopies) were ordered for the two platforms in October 1891 and the work was duly carried out over the following eighteen months at a cost of £2,600. The straight bore of Werneth tunnel is clear of any smoke, quite a change from just over a decade earlier when due to the lack of ventilation a fog hung in the place for most of the time. The station buildings were demolished in 1970, replaced by an unstaffed halt.

A. J. Cocker.

Werneth station 1953. The first in Oldham, Werneth opened in 1842. Simple in design, the booking hall was furnished for some reason with rather tall doors which was about the only touch of extravagance afforded the place. The booking hall spanned the tracks and formed the bridge linking the two platforms. Originally the platforms and tracks were covered with a single all–over roof but this was dismantled during the alterations of the 1880–1890s. It must have been a grand place indeed when first opened but no doubt outlived its purpose to have been taken down only forty–odd years later. One theory is that because of the low clearance smoke and steam from locomotives became something of a nuisance.

British Railways.

Werneth booking hall in 1969, except for the strip lighting above the stairway the place is virtually unchanged from those far off days of the 1840s.

A. J. Cocker.

Fowler 0–8–0 7F No.49515 struggles up the last few feet of the climb from Hollinwood, on the 12th May 1956, with a loaded goods train from that place and probably bound for Moston via Rochdale. Loads for Oldham from the Manchester direction usually ran via Rochdale to be tripped from Royton Junction, otherwise goods trains via Failsworth would require a banker. About 1963 goods trains were rerouted through Failsworth and many trains required that extra push.

A. J. Cocker.

The gated railway entrance to Platt Brothers works in June 1963. Just like the tracks in the foreground, much of Platts was now derelict or in decline. The roadbridge girder, on the right, bears testimony to the early days of Britain's growing industrial might and Oldham's forthcoming prosperity — 1842. The left hand section of the bridge, over the BR running lines, was new provided for the widening of the railway when the new line from Thorpes Bridge via Hollinwood was opened, forming a new junction here in May 1880.

T. A. Fletcher.

Looking down the inclines, November 1956. Branching off to the left is the Hollinwood line with a fairly stiff gradient of 1 in 50 and straight on is the Werneth incline proper with the steepness of the 1 in 27 quite apparent, dropping away alarmingly. Just behind the platform on the left can be seen one of the small goods sheds that first served the area. The bridge abutment on the same platform was built on part of the site of the original station masters house, demolished during the station alterations of 1883/84; on the bridge itself are the signals controlling the junction.

Authors collection.

Stanier 2–6–4T No.42654 starts away from Werneth with the 5.40 p.m. Manchester Victoria – Rochdale, 18th May 1958.

A. J. Cocker.

Spanning the tracks at the west end of the station was this footbridge erected in the spring of 1884 at a cost of £433 15/-. It was put in during alterations to the station and linked up with the long footbridge leading from the Featherstall Road entrance, erected some years earlier. All the footbridges were taken down in 1970. Point rodding and signal wires, from Werneth No.1 box, control the junction, whilst on the right, can be seen part of the garden tended by the men from that box. 20th November 1956.

Authors collection.

The famous gradient post at the west end of the down platform, informing all and sundry, and especially footplate crews, that here was the top of the steepest main line gradient in Britian.

A. J. Cocker.

Former L&YR 2–4–2T No.50647 and A Class 0–6–0 No.52438 haul the joint tour organised by the Manchester Locomotive Society and the Stephenson Locomotive Society *Old Manchester Railtour* up the last few yards of the Werneth Incline on 12th May 1956.

A. J. Cocker.

The 'continuous pilot coal stage' outside the tunnel entrance. These stages, with their supply of coal, enabled pilot or yard engines to stay away from their home sheds for up to a week at a time; usually a fresh engine would arrive for work early on a Monday morning to shunt the yard until about the following Saturday afternoon when it would return to its home shed – Newton Heath in this case – for the locomotives boiler to be washed out and any mechanical maintenance to be performed. Crews of course would be relieved at the end of their normal hours of duty but the engine would, if the yard was particularly busy, work round the clock calling at the stage for coal when required. Water was supplied from the parachute tank positioned at the end of the Down platform. It was erected in 1885 at a cost of £231, its appearance probably coinciding with the building of the coal stage. The L&Y were one of the few companies to use this particular method of 'continuous' operation and of the 33 such stages employed throughout their system this example was one of two found in the Oldham area; the other was at Royton Junction. The tiny signalbox (Werneth No.2) was really only a glorified covered groundframe controlling the entrance to the yards on either side of the main line. As can be seen, in June 1959, half its workload is already gone, the track of the yard on the south side of the station having been lifted. By this date the coal stage seems to have become a p.w. and S & T store. The locomotive, on the 2.26 p.m. Mumps to Blackpool and Fleetwood, is Class 5 No.44696.

A. J. Cocker.

With less than two months to go before steam was banished from BR a Stanier Class 5 4–6–0 No.44949, of Newton Heath shed, and banked at the rear by a Type 2 diesel, brings a coal train for Higginshaw gas works up to Oldham the hard way via the Hollinwood branch. With half its train on the level stretch of track through the station the mixed traffic locomotive gets ready for some more difficult work on the climb up to Mumps through Werneth and Central tunnels.

A. J. Cocker.

A deserted scene on March 1968 with a fence marking the course of the incline. The view today is very different; gone are the platform canopies, footbridge, booking hall, waiting rooms and the extra large gap between the running lines. The platforms have been realigned with bus stop type shelters serving the waiting passengers and the only access now, from Featherstall Road, is by path from stairways off the original 1842 roadbridge. Notice the two recently erected concrete piers beneath the original bridge.

A. J. Cocker.

The Oldham bound Down platform (No.2) on 30th March 1968.

The first of the Werneth goods yards was situated on a rather cramped site between the line and Railway Road. The yard did though boast two small (by Oldham standards) goods sheds served by wagon turntables. The growth of the cotton industry soon brought this yard to the point of saturation and by 1874 plans were being drawn up to build a much larger complex on the north side of the line beyond the Werneth coal yard and West Street, to be served by a short branch line. It was however to be another twelve years before sufficient land was available to enable completion of the project. The two warehouses built in 1887/8, to cater for the expanding cotton industry, stood in the new Werneth goods station. The yard, tucked away out of sight from the main line, was bordered on the north side by Middleton Road with Featherstall Road to the west; a high embankment topped by rows of terraced housing on the town side restricted any further expansion. The L&Y experienced great difficulty during the late 1870s in securing properties, so much so that it had to apply for an extension of the Act of 1875. The little branch line, running under West Street, connecting the yard with the main line at Werneth station was closed in October 1966, the yard itself having become redundant and closing some months earlier. A gong was fixed in Werneth tunnel for the purpose of communicating with goods train drivers wishing to set back into the yard. The simple instructions were: 1 beat, Stop; 2 beats, Set back; 3 beats, Draw ahead; 4 beats (for guards only) release brake. This last instruction enabled wagons to be brought into the yard by gravity. *(top)* Werneth goods yard looking south west from the unloading platform in 1932. Empty baskets and packing cases are stacked awaiting return to the numerous cotton mills in the area to which they belonged. Just to the left of the nearest gas lamp is West Street bridge through which the short branch line from Werneth station connected this complex with the main line. The overhead travelling crane, running on its massive timber gantry, was of 10 tons capacity; steam powered, it was made by the L&Y at Miles Platting works and numbered 1778 in the L&Y register. Beyond the crane is the sorting shed where goods of all kinds were classified for local distribution or warehousing in the adjacent five storey sundry warehouse. The huge sundries building replaced a similar sized structure burnt down in 1891. The original warehouse was only three years old when disaster struck after having cost over £24,000 with its adjacent sidings. The later building, as can be seen, was erected with a party wall dividing each floor and extending through the roof. Behind the sundries warehouse is the cotton warehouse built, with conflagration in mind, at a distance from the taller building. The array of private owner wagons have brought coal from all parts of the country; in addition to this yard, another large minerals yard was located just beyond West Street bridge with vehicular access from Featherstall Road. *(bottom)* The view looking north west, towards Middleton Road, on the same day, shows further detail of the buildings and structures associated with this typical ex–L&YR goods station. Again private owner wagons dominate this end of the yard.

V. R. Anderson collection.

Towards the end of steam on British Railways, which incidentally coincided with the closure of many lines and installations, enthusiast groups regularly organised special trains over threatened lines with requested locomotives. The remains of Werneth goods yard saw one such special on the 7th August 1965 when Fowler 2–6–4T No.42343 brought a train of brakevans, with LCGB members entrained, around the curve at the rear of Werneth station.

A. J. Cocker.

BR/Sulzer Type 2 diesel–electric D7506 (later class 25) brings a short parcels train into Werneth station en route to Clegg Street on the 30th March 1968.

A. J. Cocker.

The east end of Werneth station on the 18th May 1968 with BR/Sulzer Type 2 D5066 (later class 24) hauling a train of empty parcel vans to Clegg Street. On the right can be seen the derelict mineral yard. The dark satanic surroundings of the station reflect the Oldham of old when *muck meant brass* and nobody really cared about the environment.

A. J. Cocker.

To celebrate the passing of the Werneth Incline a brake van special was organised by the Locomotive Club of Great Britain, to traverse the line on the 5th January 1963 filled to capacity with enthusiasts paying their last respects to the doomed railway. The engine, Stanier 8F 2–8–0 No.48546, was nicely turned out for the occasion but things did not run smoothly; ice on the rails had the huge engine slipping to a halt a number of times eventually stalling on the 1 in 27 gradient. Assistance was summoned and a WD Austerity 2–8–0 No.90526 pushing at the rear helped the 8F on its way. Here the detrained enthusiasts look on as the WD lends its muscle to the struggle. Shortly after this photograph was taken the 8F suddenly found its feet and, with the added power of the WD, the train accelerated alarmingly and detrained enthusiasts had to dash to board the brake vans before they were left behind. The last passenger train down the Werneth Incline on that date was the 5.50 a.m. ex Rochdale.

A. J. Cocker.

Looking up the abandoned incline in July 1963 towards the heart of the Platts empire. It was just below this point where a short branch led off to the Chamber Colliery Co. Stockfield mine. A brick built signalbox was erected in 1883 to control movements from the new branch sidings, called incidentaly Incline Siding, to both the Up and Down lines; BoT inspector Major General Hutchinson inspected the work in April 1883 and reported ....*these connections which join both Up and Down lines are worked by interlocked levers in a new signal cabin, properly carried out except for one or two minor details...* Subject to those minor details sanction was given to operate the box. The siding connection was dismantled in 1919 when the 'pit' was worked out. At the same time the colliery connection was laid a new siding was also put into the works of Messrs Platts and part of the by now severed connection can be seen on the left. Notice what appears to be newly laid ballast on the Incline; this 'new look' is caused by acid rain which cleans off oily deposits and suchlike, from the limestone.

T. A. Fletcher.

Messrs. Platts New Hartford works from bridge No. 34, over Suthers Street, on the Hollinwood branch in March 1957. On the extreme left can be seen some goods wagons standing on a siding beside 'the Incline'. Terraced housing, their roofs just visible beyond the bridge parapet, stand in the wye of the junction of the Hollinwood and Middleton Junction lines, in an area known as Alder Root.

Authors collection.

The goods branch to Chadderton was opened in August 1914 and has only recently fallen into disuse. Coal was the main commodity brought to the yard at Broadway and up until the early 1980s the company operating the yard employed their own locomotives to do the sorting and shunting. In September 1960 the Roch Valley Railway Enthusiasts Society organised a special train utilising two former L&YR locomotives – very popular then around this part of the world for such events – whose itinerary included traversing the goods only branch to Chadderton coal yard. This was the only time that coaching stock went to Chadderton and on the lightly used metals with their four coach train are 2P 2–4–2T No.50850 and 3F 0–6–0 No.52271.

J. Davenport.

Having just passed under Broadway bridge, at the foot of the Werneth Incline, Stanier 2–6–4T No.42565 hurries its train, the 5.25 p.m. from Rochdale, towards Middleton Junction. 27th May 1958.

A. J. Cocker.

HOLLINWOOD.

Hollinwood station frontage in June 1969, little changed from opening.

A. J. Cocker.

To gain entrance to the platforms from the booking hall one had to proceed through this subway (bridge No.25 on the branch), brightly lit here by the camera flash but normally a gloomy place where small children would leap into their parents arms if a train happened to be going over whilst they were passing through. This 1958 view shows that the pad stones are in need of attention, little wonder considering the pressures exerted on them over the previous seventy–odd years.

Authors collection.

Opened on the 17th May 1880, Hollinwood station was part of a contract started in mid 1875 to provide an alternative and easier route to Oldham from Manchester. Costing in excess of £153,000, the new route had three stations; Dean Lane, Failsworth and Hollinwood which was also furnished with a goods warehouse erected at a cost of £3,500. Immediately after opening, traffic on the Middleton Junction–Werneth line was halved although certain passenger trains still maintained a through service from Manchester to Oldham. Besides having prize–winning gardens on both platforms in 1962, Hollinwood station did look a tidy place considering it was surrounded by foundries, mills and factories. The staff were no doubt a conscientious lot justly proud of their place of work and the township of Hollinwood itself with its industrial heritage. Part of the garden on the down side greeted the traveller from Manchester with the message, depicted in flowers, HOLLINWOOD FOR INDUSTRY. Todays traveller to Hollinwood is greeted with the scourge of unstaffed stations – urban graffiti.

Oldham Evening Chronicle.

The L&Y never did spend extravagantly, especially on the Hollinwood branch. Timber platform buildings would suffice. Down side buildings in 1964.

Authors collection.

The view towards Oldham on a typical showery day in October 1958. The skyline has changed somewhat since then and there are no canopies to shelter under; two small, vandalised, bus shelters are deemed sufficient. The signalbox, with its 48 lever Horwich built frame, is now only operational during the morning and evening rush periods and only about a third of the original levers are required. At least there is still a train service.

Authors collection.

Newton Heath A Class 0–6–0 No. 12138 shunting the yard behind the station in late August 1949. Looking at the mess in the tender passing itself off as coal one can only have sympathy for the fireman.

A. J. Cocker.

Bower Lane passes beneath Hollinwood station by way of this bridge which is infamous locally as one with a fatal attraction for double decker buses. Despite the warning notices, double deckers still try to travel through the restricted opening even though they are nearly a foot higher than the available headroom. Over the years more than a dozen buses have tried and failed, ending up as open top vehicles; the bridge of course hasn't budged. Meanwhile the railway got on with business and on the notice board is offering return excursion fares of seven shillings (35p) to Blackpool Illuminations. The date – 2nd October 1958.

Authors collection.

Stanier Class 5 No. 44916 passes Hollinwood warehouse in late July 1967 with a parcels train for Crewe, its previous route via the OA&GB now closed.

A. J. Cocker.

Behind the Up side platform at Hollinwood these goods lines kept shunting trains away from the running lines whilst they went about their business day in and day out. A BR Standard Class 4, something of a rarity on goods trains at this time, goes about sorting its train in the goods yard in October 1958.

Authors collection.

Diesel electric Class 40 No.40174 roars through Hollinwood on the 6th March 1979 with a Brighton & Hove Albion Football Club four coach team special, bound for Werneth. Included in the make-up of the train was a modern Metro–Cammell Pullman car used by the Brighton team whenever they played away from home.

R. S. Greenwood.

OLDHAM CENTRAL.

The staggered platforms looking towards Central tunnel, 24th September 1964. Built for the opening of the line from Werneth to Mumps in November 1847, the station was rebuilt during 1865–66 at a cost of £7,600, the main job being to off set the platforms so that the southerly one did not encroach onto those of the recently opened Clegg Street station. The architecture is pure L&Y with cast iron columns supporting the ornate canopy; stone flags form the platform surface and the buildings are all brick rather than stone built. Situated as it was next to Clegg Street, Central could easily be mistaken by the unaware traveller to be one and the same.

British Railways.

East end of Central on August 3rd 1964 looking towards Waterloo sidings. The only real sign of the diesel age are the two notices on the Down platform informing drivers of two and four car dmus where to stop. The canopy ends were taken down at an unknown date but otherwise the station remains as it was a century before. Between the running lines, in the 'six–foot', stand the 'monuments' those simple yet essential devices found on curves enabling the p.w. engineers to align the track in parallel.

J. J. Smith.

The rather grand booking office of Central situated in a small square at the juncture of Wellington Street and Clegg Street. The date is early February 1953, with a smattering of what comes naturally to Oldham at that time of the year. Posters advertise cheap trips for football and rugby fans to Rochdale on the same day, 21st February. Another poster beckons the non-sporting types with an evening trip to Blackpool for five shillings and nine pence. Bovril on the terraces sounds more enticing than a walk on the windy Prom!

Thompson Collection.

BR Standard Class 4 2–6–4T No.80093 pulls away from Central with an afternoon train from Manchester to Rochdale in 1956. When the class 4 tank was ousted by dmus from Newton Heath to Blackpool shed in the late 1950s, it was still a regular visitor to Oldham and would often be seen at the head of the 4.37 p.m. from Middleton Junction to Rochdale. This train would then form the 5.42 p.m. Rochdale to Blackpool but was not advertised as running from Oldham.

J. Davenport.

A pair of Hughes/Fowler 'Crabs', Nos. 42728 and 42871, burst out of Central tunnel with a Good Friday excursion from Oldham to Liverpool in 1960.

P. Hutchinson.

The new order of local trains – a Metropolitan–Cammell two car dmu enters Central on a service from Royton in 1958.

J. Davenport.

Central station thawing out after overnight snow 3rd April 1966. The station was to close some two weeks later, on the same day as the Royton branch, 18th April.

T.A.Fletcher.

CLEGG ST & THE O.A.&.G.B.

A busy scene at Clegg Street in June 1952 with C13 No. 67438, having just arrived from Guide Bridge and almost ready to continue its journey to Glodwick Road. In the far platform a motor–fitted Fowler 2–6–2T *breadvan* No.40056 waits to depart with a Delph train. Central station's booking office can be seen above the Fowler tank giving some idea of the close proximity of the two stations. In the period before Grouping trains ran from here to Manchester London Road and from 1909 to Manchester Central station. Early motive power consisted of Manchester Sheffield & Lincolnshire 2–4–0 well tanks, these being supplanted by 2–4–2 tanks from the 1890s and the final MS&L/Great Central contribution was the mainstay of the line's motive power until closure, Robinson's elegant 4–4–2 tanks. LNWR trains over the route in those far off days were handled by 2–4–2 tanks and 0–6–0 tender engines of both Ramsbotton and Webb designs, Manchester Longsight shed providing them until both Lees and Stockport Edgeley were built. The little shed at Mumps came to have insufficient space, even after being lengthened, to house all that were required.

J. Davenport.

In BR days Lees shed was responsible for most of the passenger services to Stockport and usually provided 2–6–4 tanks but it was not unusual to find a former Lanky 'A' Class 0–6–0 on this service. 52427 works the empty stock off the 12.34 p.m. ex Stockport onto the sidings at Clegg Street in 1954.

J. Davenport.

The last C13 4–4–2T No. 67417, spent its remaining days working the OA&GB push–pull service and is at the head of one such working after arrival from Guide Bridge on a morning train in late May 1958. Until three years previously, the train would have continued on to Glodwick Road, to terminate in the bay platform there but upon closure of that station in April 1955, the Guide Bridge service was forced to reverse at Clegg Street.

P. Hutchinson.

On the same day the C13 is propelling its stock back into Clegg Street to form the 12.10 p.m. service to Guide Bridge. The front vehicle is one of Gresley's Great Northern suburban coaches far from its usual stomping ground in north London, the legend on the left hand side beneath the window proclaiming *ALEXANDRA PALACE PUSH & PULL*. C13s from Gorton shed were the mainstay motive power on the OA&GB trains but in its last year of operation and with the 4–4–2Ts ailing, Gorton would sometimes provide a Thompson L1 2–6–4 tank hauling just one coach. Diesel multiple units would probably have been ideal for the service but alas they were never tried. The line from Oldham Clegg Street to Ashton and Guide Bridge closed to passengers from 4th May 1959 with the last train fittingly hauled by a C13.

P. Hutchinson.

One of the coach sets used on the Delph branch, Open Trailer M3423 and Motor Coach M3414, parked under the footbridge in Clegg Street goods yard 2nd April 1955.

A.J.Cocker.

The south end of Clegg Street in April 1959 with 67417 hardly taxing itself as it leaves on the 1.40 p.m. service to Guide Bridge. Long gone is the milk hoist but more noticeable is the look of sheer dereliction that had overtaken the place, even before the impending closure.

A.J.Cocker.

Opposite. Oldham Clegg Street was the largest of the five railway stations situated within the Borough of Oldham. Rebuilt during the period 1899 to 1901, it had four platforms and was the only station in Oldham to boast refreshment facilities, the license for these being granted in 1880 to a Mr John Felton. At the south end was a 'milk bridge' costing £1,000 complete with hydraulic half–ton capacity lifts serving the platforms and a milk stage. Two one ton luggage lifts were situated in the central area of the station, the tower containing the hydraulic equipment rising alongside the street level booking office. It was from here that the OA&GB operated a horse–drawn omnibus service to Rochdale via Royton commencing in September 1861 but ceasing just two years later when the L&Y opened their line to Rochdale via Shaw & Crompton. From opening Clegg Street had drawn business passengers wishing to connect with London trains at Stockport. Facilities were, even with the refreshment room, getting a bit tatty as early as the late 1880s and in August 1889 the Oldham Town Clerk sent a letter to the OA&GB Board complaining....*of the lack of accomodation at Clegg Street Station*...Nothing of course was done at the time but some eight years later in July 1897 the matter of rebuilding Clegg Street was discussed by the LNWR who ....*wished to avoid the kind of expenditure involved*... The estimate for the job amounted to over twenty thousand pounds but eventually sanction was given to rebuild the station, the General Manager being asked to get some money off Oldham Corporation for part of the bridge renewal. The total cost of rebuilding Clegg Street was some £20,445 made up as follows:- 'Permanent Way £1,488, New Platforms £5,150, Retaining and Wharf wall £2,090, Buildings £5,030, New Bridge carrying Clegg Street £4,867, Water Supply £320, Signalling £500, Bridge, Stage and Hoists for Milk Traffic £1,000.' In August 1964, after five years of closure, Clegg Street station was still very much intact although canopies and the platform copings on the remaining through roads have been removed probably to give greater clearance and the bays and platforms are weed ridden. The street level milk stage and its associated hoists and bridge are long gone but the station was to remain derelict like this for many years before redevelopment of the area saw the cuttings filled in and all vestiges of the railway swept away, to provide for retail shopping units.

J. J. Smith.

Clegg Street frontage in December 1955. The less than inviting building is brightened only by the advertising; post–war dilapidation had set in with a vengeance with broken windows and a glassless canopy over the entrance. The ornate window frames above the doors might have been subject to a preservation order today indeed the whole station would probably be looked upon as typical of Edwardian enterprise and optimism.

British Railways.

Stanier Class 4MT 2–6–4T No.42551 of Lees shed moves empty stock off Waterloo sidings to form a Clegg St–Stockport train in 1958.

J. Davenport.

the great variety of wagons filling the sidings but also in the surrounding buildings. Immediately behind the wagons is the original Clegg Street station complete with its overall roof, devoid of any glazing except for that topping the smoke ventilator on the ridge. What a miserable place it must have been in those days. The tower containing the hydraulic apparatus has yet to to built so too, has the footbridge, linking Clegg Street with Woodstock Street (remains of stone steps still intact at Woodstock St end, 1991). The range of buildings nearest the camera house from left to right – the refreshment room, 1st class dining room, gentlemens and ladies 1st class waiting rooms, as well as general waiting rooms. The promoters of the OA&GB certainly had some big ideas when this station was planned. The L&Y get into the picture with Central station booking office standing just above Clegg St, and just discernable on the left is the eastern portal of Central tunnel, with Wellington mill above it. The Manchester Sheffield & Lincolnshire Railway goods warehouse commands its own position on the extreme left with its numerous drays and newly built office block overseeing the apparent chaotic scene. The wagons in view are mainly dumb–buffered types with private firms, including local ones, outnumbering the few railway company examples, represented by the Great Northern and L&NWR. Shortage of siding space seems to have been neatly overcome in two cases, with wagons off the rails. Coal and lime, the latter for both building and sanitation use, appear to be the main cargos. Huge baulks of timber and stone blocks can be seen on the left, no doubt destined for some cotton mill in the making. This was the age of expansion for the cotton industry and the railways were responsible for transporting virtually everything that was required, from building materials to the raw cotton bales. Just out of view on the left is the elegant curved warehouse of the L&NWR.

Oldham MBC Local Studies Library.

Clegg Street Parcels Concentration Depot 30th August 1960. A new beginning and hope for Oldham's railways. The depot built on the site of the former Clegg St goods yard was designed to handle parcels traffic emanating from the various mail–order company warehouses that had taken over so many redundant cotton mills. To enable quick dispatch to all parts of the country, the OA&GB line was given a new lease of life handling up to eight trains a day to destinations as varied as Hayes in Middlesex and Carlisle to the north. Stanier class 5s were the staple motive power for these trains, empty vans would be returned during the day to be stored on Clegg Street or Glodwick Road yards and when required would be shunted into the depot and made up into trains. Diesel shunters were inevitably employed on the shunting jobs with various types tried out over the years, from the diminutive D28XX 0–4–0 to the ubiquitous 08 0–6–0 diesel electric, although a steam locomotive would occasionally be used when the sole diesel was away for repair. Sadly Clegg Street PCD is now no longer with us – it closed in 1982 due to the fierce competition from road transport and, reportedly, an unfortunately high incidence of pilfering.

E. M. Johnson.

Besides dispatching literally thousands of parcels every week, Clegg Street PCD received a significant if somewhat lesser amount in return. This view shows a batch of the 'forwarded' parcels being loaded into a General Utility Van (GUV) shortly after the depot was opened. The road vehicle is one of the universal BR 'mechanical horses' used in this instance only within the depot confines, hence the lack of registration plates. Newton Heath shed provided the diesel shunter standing outside.

British Railways.

Seen from Goddard Street bridge, just south of Clegg Street station, ex Lanky 0–6–0 No. 52410 nears the end of its journey with a train from Stockport in August 1957. Notice the neatness of the permanent way. In February 1885 a memorial was received from the residents of the Honeywell Lane area asking for a station to be erected nearby. After the passenger services were withdrawn from the OA&GB it got another lease of life, for a short period, when trains from and to the new parcels concentration depot (PCD) at Clegg Street used the line to gain access to national routes.

J. Davenport.

Stanier Class 5 No. 44933, of Newton Heath, pilots Jubilee No. 45670 *HOWARD OF EFFINGHAM* down the 1 in 86 from Honeywell Lane bridge, towards Park Bridge with a Newcastle – Liverpool Lime St express, in May 1953. This Sunday working was diverted through Oldham because engineering work on its usual route through Stalybridge had closed the line for the day.

J. Davenport.

Fowler 4F 0–6–0 No. 44379 of Buxton shed and Jubilee No. 45623 *PALESTINE* of Longsight shed darken the sky of Fitton Hill at the start of the 1 in 86 gradient up to Clegg St with a Newquay – Castleton relief in August 1952. Scenes such as this were commonplace on the OA&GB during those post–war summers when trains used the route to gain access to the mill towns east of Manchester, leaving the main line at Stockport.

J. Davenport.

Fowler 2–6–2T 40062 climbs past Snipe Clough on a cold March day in 1952 with the 12.34 p.m.(Saturdays only) train from Stockport to Clegg St. After terminating the stock would be stabled in Waterloo sidings, the engine returning to Lees for servicing.

J. Davenport.

BR Standard Cl.2 2–6–2T No. 84015 crosses over near Sheepwashers Lane signalbox on the 2nd April 1955, ready to work back to Delph engine first. The stock is made up of Open Trailer M3427 and Motor Coach M3416. The service that brought this formation here was the 12.06 p.m. ex–Delph.

A. J. Cocker.

Below. A returning holiday period train from Newquay to Castleton on the 20th August 1960 tackles the final part of the climb along the OA&GB into Oldham. Motive power is provided by two Hughes/Fowler 'Crabs' Nos. 42848 and 42815.

P. Hutchinson.

C13/3 67421 propels its train across the viaduct, towards Park Bridge, on its way to Guide Bridge on 13th April 1957.

J. Davenport.

67417 crossing Park Bridge viaduct with the 3.40 p.m. Guide Bridge – Oldham Clegg Street train, 2nd April 1959. The viaduct was refurbished in 1960 for the anticipated heavy parcels traffic emanating from Oldham parcels depot. Track bed was taken up, ballast and fill from the top of the arches discarded and concrete poured into the voids. The new ballast was laid along with track to await the increased demand which in the event never materialised. Some half dozen trains a day used the route but, by 1967, it was found to be more of a luxury than an asset and the line between Ashton and Oldham was closed. In 1970 the track was taken up and in the following spring Park Bridge viaduct was demolished, ending just over a hundred years history of the Oldham Ashton & Guide Bridge Railway.

A. J. Cocker.

Park Bridge station looking north, about the turn of the century.

Tameside Libraries.

An evening service, 4.31 p.m. ex Huddersfield to Stockport via Oldham brought some variety to the OA&GB besides the usual Oldham–Stockport or Guide Bridge trains. Fairburn 2–6–4T No. 42114, a Lees engine, slows to pick up passengers in the late summer of 1954.

J. Davenport.

Park Bridge signalbox with a Fowler *breadvan* arriving from Stockport, in 1954. The station nameboard displays Parkbridge as one word whereas that on the box is split.

J. Davenport.

C13/3 No. 67417 entering Park Bridge from the Oldham direction with an evening train to Guide Bridge, on the last day of April 1959. By now a one coach train was sufficient to maintain the meagre passenger loadings with the imminent withdrawal of passenger services just days away. The main station building is neglected, indeed it is probable that BR never did maintain the place for any degree of permanence. The last lick of paint must have been pre–war although the ridge tiles on the roof and the chimney seem to have had some attention, more likely repairs from storm damage than preventive maintenance. Within a year of closure the buildings were badly damaged by fire as a result of vandalism but they had stood unbowed for nearly a century, which in the case of timber structures seems remarkable, to say the least.

P. Hutchinson.

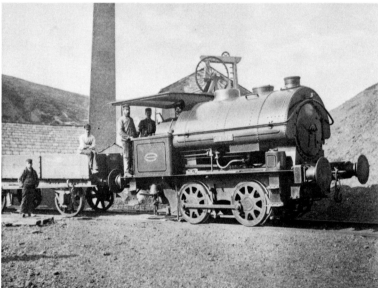

Park Bridge station 2nd May 1959, and the final day of the passenger service. Old faithful C13 67417 calls on its way to Guide bridge with the 4.22 p.m. ex–Clegg Street. The timber built Oldham platform is suffering from settling or subsidence along the whole of its length, possibly due to coal workings at the nearby Wood Park colliery. On the right is the spur leading through the small goods yard to the ironworks.

A.J.Cocker.

At Park Bridge there was an iron works belonging to Hannah Lees & Sons where a small rail system kept two Beyer Peacock inside cylinder 0–4–0 saddle tank locomotives employed for many years. In keeping with most industrial concerns the engines were named, *ORION* BP 3020 of 1889 and *PEGASUS* BP 4320 of 1901. Here we see *ORION* in splendid condition about 1900.

Authors collection.

42551, one of the highly regarded Stanier 2–6–4 tanks gets its load underway across the viaduct after the stop for Park Bridge. The rough cut stone of the viaduct is well depicted in this view. Also to be seen, in the background, are the sidings of the ironworks with a self–propelled steam crane going about its business, 1957.

J. Davenport.

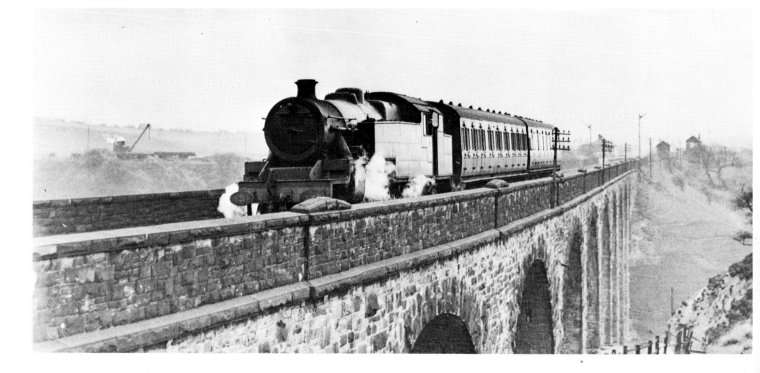

AROUND CENTRAL OLDHAM.

Stanier Class 5 No.44677 draws a van train for Carnforth out of the parcels depot on a summers evening in June 1967. The new, 55 lever, Oldham Mumps signalbox in the background is now fully operational having taken on all the signalling requirements for the central Oldham area, replacing Mumps Nos 1, 2 and 3, Sheepwashers Lane, Waterloo Sidings and Werneth.

P. Hutchinson.

Evening activity at Clegg Street PCD in July 1967.
J. Davenport.

The former L&NWR goods shed at Clegg Street in 1985. The building still survives today more than 125 years after its completion. A preservation order has been placed upon it because of its unique curving design; however the fabric of the structure is in urgent need of repair and various time-wasting schemes over recent years have done nothing to speed along the much needed restoration.
Oldham Evening Chronicle.

In May 1974 with parcels still big business BR/Sulzer Class 25 diesel electrics 25050 and 25209 await their evening departures from Glodwick Road yard. In the background an electricity sub–station stands on the site of the erstwhile Oldham Corporation Greenhill electricity generating station. In the left background the soon to be demolished Greenbank mills stand as a stark reminder of the past.

P. Hutchinson.

In April 1966 ex–LMS 3F 0–6–0T No.47383 shunts empty vans. This 'Jinty' is now amongst the preserved stock on the Severn Valley Railway. The footbridge is Gas Street from where our imaginery journeys began.

R. S. Greenwood.

BR Standard No.80088 passing under Gas Street footbridge with a Rochdale – Manchester Victoria train in 1955. The first proposal to build a bridge here appears to have surfaced in 1882 and it seems that by early 1884 work was well advanced when a great storm blew down the structure on the 2nd February. No doubt the replacement was much more substantial and that same footbridge stands today, cleaned and painted, as a memorial to the time when the railway played such a part in the greatness of this country.

J. Davenport.

The maze of lines spanned by Gas Street footbridge are well depicted in this late July 1963 view of Stanier Class 5s Nos.45339 and 44816 effortlessly hauling a Sunday excursion of non–corridor stock away from Central towards Mumps. The pilot engine would be removed at Rochdale.

R. S. Greenwood.

The last steam hauled passenger train through Oldham was this enthusiasts railtour in 1968, hauled by Stanier 8F 2–8–0 No.48476 and BR Standard Class 5 No.73069. Although British Railways banned steam locomotive haulage after August 1968, they subsequently relented and allowed preserved steam onto certain routes; however the Oldham loop which sees the occassional diesel–hauled railtour has yet to be traversed by preserved steam. The route through Hollinwood to Werneth especially would guarantee a pyrotechnics display not seen for some twenty odd years. Compare this and the above photograph which were taken from the same spot but five years apart. many buildings had gone, so had some of the signalling and of course the OA&GB lines. Many more changes have occured here since 1968 and a stroll over Gas Street footbridge will reveal all.

J. Davenport.

Even WD 2–8–0s used to get in some passenger haulage during the Wakes holiday period although 90564 is now in charge of empty stock only as its traverses the OA&GB lines past Waterloo sidings in July 1955. The Austerity would have brought its train, a Skegness – Oldham Clegg Street relief, from Guide Bridge and is now taking it for stabling at Lightbowne carriage sidings, near Newton Heath, via Rochdale.

J. Davenport.

From Gas Street bridge the photographer could get some excellent shots of passing trains and the general layout of the railway in this the central area of Oldham. With much of the original signalling still in place as well as the old and new signal boxes a diesel multiple unit traverses the last few yards of the climb from Manchester to Oldham in 1967. The dmu, displaying Liverpool on its destination blind, was one of the Accrington based Cravens twin sets, each car powered by a single 238 b.h.p. Rolls Royce engine with hydraulic transmission. On the right is the site of the old Rhodes Bank colliery by now in use as a scrap yard for motor vehicles, an eyesore that was soon to be swept away for the by-pass (see opposite).

I. G. Holt.

Evening parcels trains, headed by Stanier Class 5 No.44949 and BR Standard No.73014, await their respective routes in the Mumps goods loops, August 1966.

J. Davenport.

Viewed from Gas Street footbridge English Electric Type 4 D239, probably the first main line diesel locomotive to visit Oldham, works the 9 a.m. Liverpool Lime Street – Newcastle express past Mumps No.1. signalbox on Sunday 9th April 1961. This train had been diverted via the OA&GB to Clegg St and thence through Glodwick Road to Greenfield because of engineering work on its usual route via Stalybridge.

J. Davenport.

Always handy as a diversionary route, Oldham has seen many long distance trains pass through when the occasion arose. This 14.28 Saturdays only Llandudno to Bradford train used the line when its usual route through Castleton was blocked by road works (building M62 motorway bridge at Castleton South Junction) on the 17th July 1971. EE Type 4 No.308 is the train engine with BR Sulzer Type 2 No.7594 serving as both pilot and extra power for the climb through Hollinwood to Werneth. On the right is the Oldham by–pass, a useful route for motorists but one which obliterated so much of the town's industrial past (perhaps for the better) including the small goods yard (Stoneyard) on the north side of Mumps station. The by–pass has isolated Mumps station from the Town Centre and left intending passengers with an obstacle course to get to it. On the left the Clegg Street PCD pilot stables for the weekend.

P. Hutchinson.

Survey of CENTRAL OLDHAM area 1932.

Scale: 1 inch = 205 feet.

Legend.

1. Site of former GCR goods warehouse.
2. Former LNWR goods warehouse (in situ 1991).
3. Clegg Street station.
4. Central station.
5. Waterloo Street bridges.
6. Gas Street footbridge.
7. Stoneyard sidings.
8. Mumps station.
9. Mumps goods yard.
10. Former L&Y goods shed.
11. Former LNWR goods shed (in situ 1991).
12. Glodwick Road station.
13. Former LNWR goods warehouse.
14. Greenhill electricity generating plant.
15. Anglo American Oil Co.

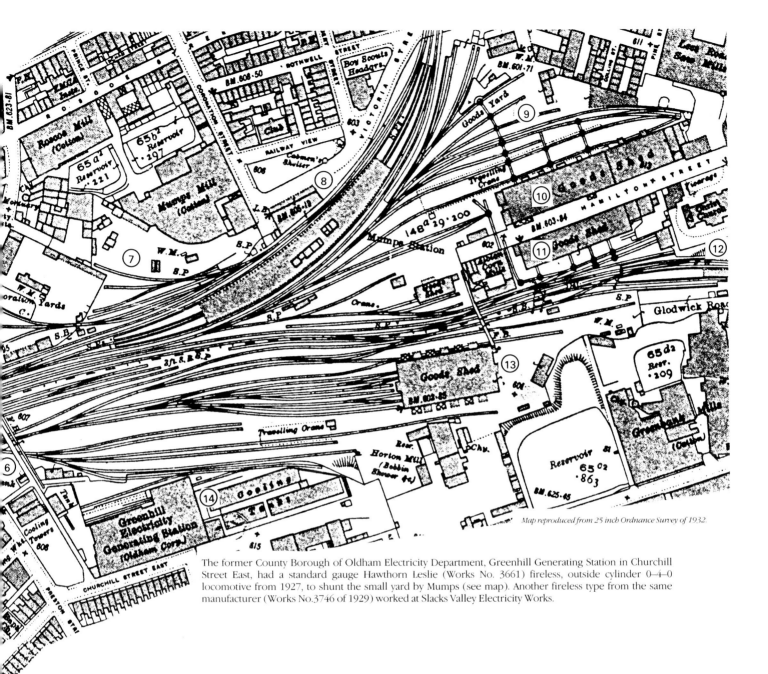

Map reproduced from 25 inch Ordnance Survey of 1932.

The former County Borough of Oldham Electricity Department, Greenhill Generating Station in Churchill Street East, had a standard gauge Hawthorn Leslie (Works No. 3661) fireless, outside cylinder 0–4–0 locomotive from 1927, to shunt the small yard by Mumps (see map). Another fireless type from the same manufacturer (Works No.3746 of 1929) worked at Slacks Valley Electricity Works.

TODAY.

What of the future for Oldham's railway? Considering that the *system* is now down to a bare minimum it is hard to visualise any more closures without complete collapse. Admitted the new halt at Derker was a nice gesture but Greater Manchester Passenger Transport Authority was responsible for its erection and, it only replaced the desolate platforms of Royton Jct. Medium distance locomotive hauled trains were a regular part of the summer timetable in 1989 but BR were hardly lavish with the stock or the destinations on offer, still it was a step in the right direction. The suburban stock varies from the modern Sprinters and somewhat unreliable Pacers to the thirty years old diesel multiple units which should have been withdrawn a decade ago. Perhaps it is a good job that the ancient dmus were not scrapped, for on some days Oldhamers would not have a train service to use. What is it that keeps the crowds away from the train? Because keep away they do. I suppose its a bit of a *Catch 22* situation.....on the side of the train there is the convenience of not having to sit in the traffic jam on the way into Manchester, you don't have to 'park–up' and the journey time from Shaw via Oldham for instance, according to the timetable is about twenty five minutes. The bus journey is long, arduous and probably more dangerous than the train and is at certain times more expensive. In winter the train is not bothered too much by snow and ice (just look out for the crowded station platforms after an overnight snowstorm). Nowadays you don't even have to queue for a ticket as the on–train conductor issues them at your seat. What does the train have against its continual usage?.....unreliability, staff shortages and breakdowns mean a cancelled train or more, derailments can result in a complete cancellation of the services. Stations are not that well sited for town centres, especially Oldham and Rochdale. Uncertainty and rumour about closure in both the short and long term do not enhance prospective passengers figures; only the diehards make the daily trek to the station wondering if it is their service that has been cancelled today. Peak–hour trains are now well–loaded but off–peak the patronage is very low. Many Oldham residents do not know that trains still run; perhaps the lack of publicity is a factor although signposts have appeared now indicating where stations are sited.

MUMPS.

Mumps station June 1956. On the right the new booking office (demolished 1991!) has still to take shape but otherwise it's business as usual. This view looking west is little different from today except that the four coach rake in the bay doesn't stable there any more, nothing can because the track has been lifted. The run–round line and adjacent sidings no longer exist as they were not needed by diesel multiple units, likewise the parachute water tank at platform end.

British Railways.

The frontage of Mumps, seen from Coronation Street in February 1953, was nothing less than ramshackle. Even British Railways admitted that something needed to be done but it was three more years before modernisation was carried out. Another relic of the past is just visible on the left by the parcels office, a horse drawn covered parcels cart. Suprisingly BR still had quite a number of these up to the late 1950s, the LMS for instance were making carts up to the Second World War and by 1947 the same company still had over 18,000 of them, plus 6,000 horses in use throughout Britain.

The mass movement of people was and still is a railway speciality and at the start of the Wakes holidays traffic from Oldham with its surrounding towns was always very heavy. Crowded platforms on Friday evenings and Saturdays were the norm and dozens of special trains would appear, from virtually every available siding in the area, to collect the holidaymakers and *whisk* them off to all points of the compass. Amongst the destinations would be Eastbourne, Scarborough, Torquay, Newquay, Llandudno, Fleetwood (for Isle of Man), Portsmouth (for Isle of Wight), Yarmouth and of course good old Blackpool. The people depicted here in 1937 have that air of expectancy and happiness about them and you can almost feel the excitement whilst they wait patiently for their trains. Because of the amount of luggage generated it was necessary to attach a goods van or two on the ends of the trains to enable all the suitcases, grips and holdalls to be got aboard. It was all very orderly and most things went smoothly, nobody complained about the state of the coaching stock or the lack of refreshment facilities, or sometimes toilets. Mumps station at that time boasted a small, though nonetheless welcome, newspaper kiosk.

Oldham Evening Chronicle.

The Up side platform with parcels, mail and a few passengers awaiting the arrival of a Manchester bound train in 1953. Advertising is still big business with virtually every vertical surface festooned. Clocks, on the other hand, seem to be lacking. But clocks mean time and time means progress, something that the railways tend to ignore until the last minute.

B. Hilton.

The first station at Mumps was a two platform affair opened in 1847 and costing £2,600. It was then the terminus of the line from Middleton Junction and was to remain so for the next sixteen years until the extension to Rochdale via Royton Junction and Shaw was completed. A goods warehouse was erected at Mumps in 1849 on the west side of the station, it was a small affair compared with the various railway goods sheds and warehouses that were to spring up around Oldham during the next fifty years but it stood in use as a cotton (what else) store until demolished in the 1950s. The nearby Rhodes Bank colliery was rail connected with the L&Y at Mumps and a mineral yard was established to import stone as well as coal from other pits of the Lancashire coalfield, such were the demands of the growing community. Mumps station underwent modernisation during 1990 and 1991. The last time this was carried out was in 1956 when the frontage of the station was demolished to make way for a new booking hall, ticket office and parcels office. The platform facilities were hardly touched then, with just a coat of paint applied to smarten the place. Perhaps the fact that Oldham, despite its size, had no direct service to the Capital,(and still does not have one) and has never been on any main line, might have had some bearing as to the lack of investment in the railway. Mumps and environs looking east from track level April 1953. A four coach suburban set stands in the bay awaiting the next mornings commuters. The signals on the right trace the course of the Greenfield line towards Glodwick Road. The large goods warehouse was still in business.

B. Hilton.

The booking hall in 1953. It was cold and draughty in winter and greenhouse hot in summer. Untidy, unkempt and unfinished. The purse that supplied the finance for the rebuilding of Mumps in the mid 1880s must have been a shallow one for the money seems to have run out before completion of the job; the timber walled booking office is fine enough, even the train departure board is grand but what happened to the ceiling? The gas lighting was standard for the period and could be found on most stations at that time (except Clegg Street). It is no wonder that the annual holiday to the seaside was so attractive to the northern industrial town dweller; just to get away from the likes of this must have brought an uplifting of the heart.

Authors Collection.

52248 the Oldham Mumps Goods Pilot in May 1957. This former 'Lanky' A Class 0–6–0 became infamous, through no fault of its own, one winter's afternoon in 1953. Apparently minding its own business, as seen here, doing very little except the occasional shunting job as Mumps pilot, 52248 was called upon to haul an Oldham Athletic Football Club supporters special to Port Vale near Stoke on Trent, for a Cup–Tie. The story goes that the engine scheduled for the job had failed with its empty stock near Rochdale and on being told by the Mumps Station Master that their train would be heavily delayed, the large throng of supporters already on the platform began to get restless, even menacing. Being an efficient railway servant and sensing a near riot on his station the Master asked Control to send him another train as soon as possible. Control informed him that his request was impossible to grant as nothing was available and that he would have to sort out the situation himself. Walking back onto the platform he saw that drastic measures would soon have to be taken, for the crowd had now become quite ugly. The coaching stock was nearby, a scratch set from Mumps sidings but what to do for an engine? There was only one course open to him, commandeer the Pilot and use that. The engine was facing the opposite way to that shown in the photograph so it would have to work tender first. After negotiating with the Lees footplate crew, who were at first reluctant, he told them that they would only have to work the train to Stockport and there they would be relieved by a fresh engine and crew; after all they didn't know the road from Stockport southwards. The 0–6–0 was of course rundown mechanically and due for works very soon hence its less than arduous task as Mumps Pilot. The Station Master not being too aware of this fact (or not wishing to be) was more than happy to see the A Class wheel its train out of the station very late but nonetheless on its way. Pulling into Stockport Edgeley the Lees men noticed the Edgeley crew on the platform end pointing and gesticulating towards the 0–6–0. Upon enquiry the unfortunates from Lees were informed that no other engine was available and the A class would have to work the train forward to its destination. The prospect of all that overtime brought a smile to the faces of the Lees driver and his fireman but they...*didn't know the road*...The Edgeley men on the other hand flatly refused to work the A class, their argument being that they were not familiar with that type of engine and anyway it was, in their opinion, only fit for the scrapyard. After much negotiation with the station authorities, control and a certain amount of barracking from the once again restless football supporters, the enginemen decided that the Lees crew would be relieved and the Edgeley men drive the engine. So far 52248 had done alright for itself so there was no reason to assume that it could not complete the task asked of it. All went well until near their destination when the tired old 0–6–0 gave up with a hot axlebox on the tender. Eventually help came from Stoke shed, 52248 was detached and the train carried on to Port Vale just in time for the supporters to watch the last twenty minutes of the second half of the match in which Latics drew. 52248 eventually got back to Lees some days later and was unofficially christened *THE PORT VALE FLYER*. The Mumps Station Master was none too popular with either the football supporters, Control and a couple of Lees enginemen. Local tradition has it that questions were later asked in the House of Commons.

J. Davenport.

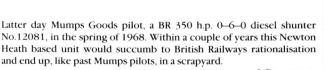

Latter day Mumps Goods pilot, a BR 350 h.p. 0–6–0 diesel shunter No.12081, in the spring of 1968. Within a couple of years this Newton Heath based unit would succumb to British Railways rationalisation and end up, like past Mumps pilots, in a scrapyard.

J. Davenport.

Stoneyard sidings at Mumps in the winter of 1961 with the chimneys of the Refuse Destructor towering over Rhodes Bank. This Sunday morning scene shows much that is no longer with us; besides the above mentioned, the Gas works and numerous smaller properties were all swept away to make room for the Oldham bypass. Mumps No.2 signalbox and the No.1, seen in the distance beneath Gas Street footbridge, became redundant on the opening of the new Oldham Mumps box in 1967. Stoneyard sidings is the site of the original Mumps goods yard dating from the opening of the line in 1847.

J. Davenport.

Mumps Goods Yard in 1961. The Beeching Report of 1963 spelt out the future for this kind of yard on British Railways – there was none, and wagon load traffic was to be overtaken by road haulage in the 1960s. The average time that a cargo spent in transit on the railways, even in the 1960s, was eight days. Road transport could virtually guarantee an overnight delivery even then without the benefit of the numerous motorways that were planned, so the future for railway goods traffic did not look too bright and installations such as Mumps Goods were in decline, closure just around the corner. Various innovations were tried by BR to win back wagonload traffic, but none of these seem to have made much difference, certainly we will never see the likes of these goods yards again unless Government money is transferred from road to rail and future administrations take on a Greener outlook. Today the Post Office Hamilton Street Sorting Office stands on this site and the only railway wagons ever seen in Oldham now are those belonging to the Civil Engineer, whenever work is required on the lines, an astonishing transformation.

J. Davenport.

A Hughes/Fowler 'Crab' No.42733 coasts into Mumps, past the No.2 signalbox, with the empty stock of a relief to Heysham, July 1961.
J. Davenport.

Seen from Waterloo Street bridge, in March 1953, ex–L&Y A Class No.52248 shunts empty stock towards Mumps station. The bridge at Waterloo St was subjected to a number of extensions or widenings over the latter years of the last century when both the L&Y and the OA&GB sought further space for their expanding operations in the central Oldham area.

J. Davenport.

The 10.36 a.m. Oldham – Blackpool 'Wakes' period special leaving Mumps on the 19th June 1971 hauled by English Electric Type 4 (later Class 40) D232 *EMPRESS OF CANADA* in green livery. The parachute tank at the platform end would still find employment, even three years after the banishment of steam locomotives, as the 40s needed to top up their train heating boiler tanks when on passenger duties. L&Y regulations for Mumps station stated, in those far off days before Grouping in 1923, that... *in wet weather and snowstorms all passenger trains must be brought to a halt under the platform canopy and if an engine requires water it must detach and draw up for that purpose.*
P. Hutchinson.

A Cravens built two–car dmu, built specially for and so long associated with the Manchester – Oldham – Rochdale route, stops at Mumps to detrain a handful of passengers on a midday service to Rochdale in June 1979. When diesel units were first introduced onto the Oldham line in February 1958 they began to take over certain of the daytime services with steam locomotives retaining a hold on the rush hour trains; by April only the latter were steam hauled and on June 8th a full diesel service was inaugurated, which saw twenty Cravens two–car units (in the M 50771–M 50817 number range) taking over all trains on the line. From Manchester there was a twenty minute service to Oldham with alternate trains thence to Rochdale or Royton. A similar 20 minute service was worked to Manchester.

R. S. Greenwood.

Civil engineering work involving the running lines is usually carried out on a Sunday and during the spring of 1963 a Lees WD 2–8–0, No.90306, gingerly reverses its engineers train past Mumps No.3 signalbox towards the work site. The bridge here, spanning Lees Road as it did then, was reconstructed during the Mumps station rebuilding of 1890–93 and then cost some £4,500 to complete.

J. Davenport.

The road to Rochdale just beyond Mumps in 1959. This section of line is little changed today except that the signals no longer exist in this form and some of the buildings in view have been demolished. It is here that trains entering Mumps from Rochdale begin the tortuous course through the curves into the platform, a slight super elevation of the track helps the cant of a train as it decelerates coming down the gradient, a check rail ensuring that the wheels stay where they should be and not where gravity wants to send them. On the right is a repeater signal, used during foggy weather to inform a fog man (a platelayer, brought in specially, and who sheltered in a tiny hut just out of view) that a train was approaching from Mumps station. The fog man would pull a lever, which controlled the rodding under the tracks in the foreground, to either place a fog detonator onto the rail or remove one with a reverse action. Now only ever used to warn approaching trains of a possible accident or breakdown, detonators were widely used until modern signalling and cab warning devices made them redundant for everyday needs. Fog, luckily, is also a rarity these days; so gone are the requirements of fogmen to spend endless, lonely, vigilant hours sat in front a brazier.

Thompson Collection.

The other side of the wall, March 1959. Subway passing under the Rochdale line and linking Bell Street with Brook Street. The rough cut stonework is typical of nineteenth century construction in the area.

GLODWICK ROAD ALONG THE WESSY.

Opened in late 1862, Glodwick Road became the permanent LNWR station in the town and replaced the temporary set–up at Mumps. Originally called Glodwick Lane, the station had two through platforms with a bay platform included in the layout from the 1880s to accommodate the OA&GB trains which terminated there. Between Glodwick Road station and Mumps, on the north side of the line and bordered by Hamilton Street, a small goods shed and a cotton warehouse completed the LNWR facilities. The goods shed was to be superseded in later years by a much larger structure, on the opposite side of the line. The LNWR operated certain of their Leeds – Stockport trains via Oldham, a practice that was carried on by the LMS. There was a four year period during the 1880s when some Leeds – Manchester expresses also used the route through Oldham and called at Clegg Street; this convenience came about through the rebuilding of the Joint station at Stalybridge. That service ceased due to the fact that double–heading of Leeds bound trains was required over the OA&GB section from Ashton, because of the heavy gradients.

Glodwick Road station 30th April 1955 with 84015 calling on the 2.35 p.m. Clegg St – Delph train. Looking towards Mumps we have the former LNWR goods warehouse dominating the scene whilst just beyond stands the original goods shed erected by the LNWR when it first reached Oldham. The signalbox is one of the LNWR oversailing types whereby the base is narrower than the actual box seated on it, a design necessary due to space limitations at ground level, in this case the proximity of the approach lines of the bay platform. Excepting the Great Western (1,646), the LNWR had the greatest number of signalboxes (1,254) of all the railways. A Fowler 7F 0–8–0 heads a short train in the goods platform bay, used at this time by Oldham Corporation, whilst alongside is the bay for trains terminating off the OA&GB. The openness of the wide curving platform at this, the west end of the station, complete with central flower bed, contrasts starkly with the claustrophobic confines of the east end.

A. J. Cocker.

Fowler 2–6–2T 40061, in early BR livery, arrives in brilliant sunshine on the 7.59 a.m. Stockport – Greenfield in June 1949.

J. Davenport.

The gloom of the east end of the closed Glodwick Road station in May 1957. The road bridge (No. 26) had recently been renewed utilising this concrete structure, the former steel girder span dating from 1890 having succumbed to the ravages of engine blast, weather and minimum maintenance. The enclosed footbridge linking the platforms is just visible in the top of the picture. During the period 1889 – 1892, Glodwick Road was subject to a programme of rebuilding, with additional facilities included in the contract. The road bridge was widened by 6 feet, Oldham Corporation putting £130 towards the total cost of £380, new general waiting room and toilets were provided on the eastbound platform, a new booking hall complete with general waiting room built at street level plus on the south platform 1st class gents and 1st and 2nd class ladies waiting rooms. The whole exercise cost in excess of £4,500.

Authors collection.

The new Glodwick Road bridge at street level in May 1957, looking towards Lees Road.

Authors collection.

A Llandudno – Greenfield relief approaches Lees past the *Glen* mill in June 1955 hauled by Stanier Class 5 No.45442. The last timetabled passenger train over this old LNWR route, 10.15 p.m. Leeds City – Oldham Clegg Street, had worked through here in the opposite direction, just weeks before on the last day of April, with a Patricroft Class 5, No.45129 doing the honours.

J. Davenport.

At the same location but a few months earlier a G2 0–8–0 No.49428 assists Ivatt 2–6–2T No.41281 on the 8.55 a.m. Glodwick Road – Delph freight. The Ivatt tank had the distinction of working the last Oldham – Delph passenger service on the 30th April 1955.

J. Davenport.

LEES.

Opened on the 5th July 1856, Lees, just over one and a half miles distant, was the first of the intermediate stations on the route to Greenfield. Enjoying a rather rural setting with moorland to the northeast and situated on the edge of the then small village of Lees, the station quietly went about its business for the next twenty two years. During that time cotton spinning in Lees, just like the whole of the Oldham area, had begun to take on a more industrious form and the need for raw cotton had prompted the railway company to provide a goods shed, for the storage and distribution of raw bales. A coal yard was laid down to serve both local coal merchants and the increasing numbers of mills. By the 1880s some of the mills adjacent to the railway had their own siding connections with the line; the Clough and Springbank mills at Springhead were two such establishments. In 1877 it was decided to build an engine shed at Lees, costing £5,500, to supersede the small shed at Mumps, which, through boundary restraints, could not be enlarged to accommodate the growing numbers of engines; Mumps shed could only house three engines though seven were actually stationed there by October 1877. In April 1879 the Locomotive Committee of the L&NWR authorised work to begin *....leveling the ground at Lees for a shed to hold twelve engines as soon as possible....* Except for losing its small and less than useless turntable at some time between the wars, nothing much happened at Lees as regards new facilities although a visit by the Locomotive Committee in June 1919 were so appalled with the toilet facilities, the nearby cess pit was overflowing, that they recommended a new water closet system costing £155 be put in immediately. The roof and shed front were in such bad repair by the early 1950s that BR were obliged to fit a new roof in 1955; at the same time opportunity was taken to cut short one of the six roads. Passenger locos were always in the minority at Lees shed, for its usual trade was the movement of coal, from the Yorkshire coalfield, and general merchandise into and out of Oldham. The fairly severe gradients in the area ensured that Lees shed always had some of the biggest and most powerful engines available for the arduous work on offer, for instance in 1917 LNWR 0–8–0s of Classes B, D and G were allocated, these types being swapped for LMS Fowler 0–8–0s during World War Two. In the late 1950s Austerity 2–8–0s had taken over the freight workings for the final years of the shed's life. On closure, 13th April 1964, the footplate staff at Lees, 28 drivers, 25 firemen and 7 cleaners, were dispered as follows; 14 drivers and 14 firemen as well as the cleaners to Newton Heath, 12 drivers and 7 firemen to the new signing–on point at Mumps station. The remainder were made redundant. The small office staff was dispersed to new posts.

Coal for the engines usually came from Cadeby colliery in Yorkshire, with occasional loads in latter days from the Lancashire pits such as Mosley Common.

The depot was transferred from the Western Division (under the supervision of Longsight, Manchester) to the Central Division in 1931 becoming C15 (under Newton Heath). Coded 26F in the 1935 LMS scheme, the code was changed in 1954 to 26E. September 1963 brought another code change, this time to 9P under Longsight once again.

By mid January 1939 the allocation was as follows:–
0–8–0: 9288, 9289, 9290, 9291, 9292, 9297.
0–6–0: 12196, 12378, 12389, 12437, 12569.
2–4–2T: 10670, 10738, 10752, 10821, 10872.
0–6–2T: 27553, 27555, 27627, 7773, 7796, 7840.
0–6–0ST: 11401, 11503.

Total 24.

31st December 1947, the last day of the LMS:-
0–8–0: 9509, 9548, 9593, 9668.
0–6–0: 12248, 12326, 12378, 12387, 12389, 12464, 12545, 12569, 12586, 12607.
2–6–4T: 2550.
2–6–2T: 12, 56, 57, 59, 60, 61, 62.

Total 22.

Notice from the above lists that the ex–LNWR G2 0–8–0s had been replaced by the less than successful LMS G3 0–8–0s (the 'Austin 7s'). Ex L&Y 0–6–0s were, by the end of the LMS period, well established having doubled their numbers during the war years. They were though, according to the Lees men, well liked and very capable engines. Other ex–Lanky types had gone never to return, as had the LNWR Coal Tanks, replaced by the Fowler 2–6–2T.

Besides local turns in the Oldham area, Lees engines would be required to shunt the yards at Ashton Oldham Road, a 7F 0–8–0 during the morning and a 3F 0–6–0 duty in the afternoon, and Royton, a WD 2–8–0 job. Another Lees job was the shunting of the yards at Royton Junction, a turn which would also involve a trip to Shaw & Crompton to shunt the goods yard there. Three Newton Heath engines, usually two ex–L&Y 0–6–0 2F tanks and a 3F 0–6–0, would travel light engine to Royton Junction each day at different times but all spending up to six hours shunting the yard and doing trips to Higginshaw gasworks and Royton goods. After World War Two the Monday morning duty of Newton Heath trip No.35, the first engine over the route, was to sand the rails on the Werneth incline whilst en route to Royton Jct. In winter this turn would sometimes require a snowplough–fitted engine to clear away the previous nights drifting snow. Diggle yard would always find employment for Lees engines at all hours of the day or night.

Lees shed, Easter Sunday 1949, with its original and rapidly decaying roof.
A. J. Cocker.

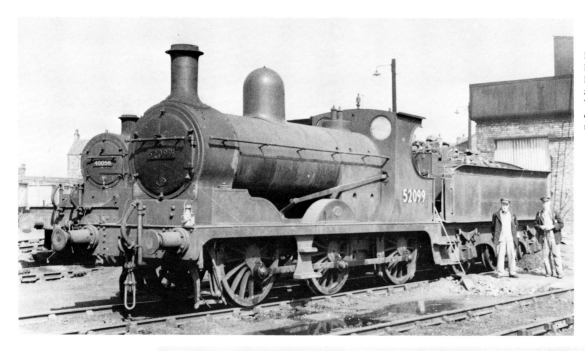

Ex L&Y 'A' class 52099 in 1952. Driver Fred Barber and firemen Frank Clark leave the engine on the ash pit after an early morning turn. The old, by now redundant, coaling stage stands to the rear of the tender.

J. Davenport.

A visiting ex–LNW 0–8–0, LMS Class G2 No. 48926 of Patricroft, waiting for a turn to take it home in 1952. These engines were for many years the mainstay of Lees heavy motive power. In the background the original northlight roof of the shed has some remedial treatment carried out, the front section was literally falling down and needed shoring up at a few points. It was to be 1955 before a new roof was eventually fitted.

J. Davenport.

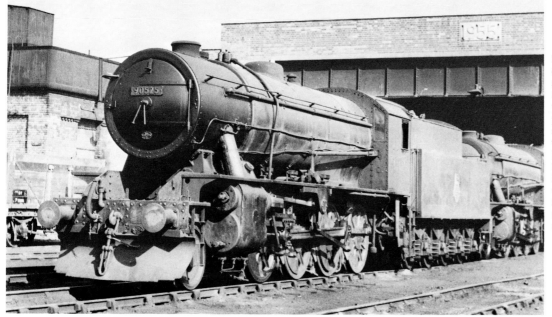

Having the luxury of two shedplates, one of which is attached to the snowplough, Austerity 2–8–0 No.90525 basks in the sun on the shed yard in 1957. It was fairly standard practice for snowploughs to have shedplates fitted, just in case they were detached from the carrying locomotive whilst it was away from home. The WDs were useful locomotives and could perform virtually any task asked of them. Heavy freight drags, pick–up goods or shunting. They could do it all and Lees certainly had them doing it.

J. Davenport.

One of the sheds 'breadvans'or 'novelties', Fowler 2–6–2 mixed traffic tank No.40061, by the new coaling stage in April 1952. Motor fitted for the Delph branch, Lees once had six of these rather unpopular engines plus two non–fitted examples, most arriving in May 1939 before the outbreak of war. They had all gone by September 1955, replaced by the superb BR Standard 2–6–2 tanks of the 84000 series and Ivatt 2–6–2T. The condition of the paintwork, typical of the period, was soon to be remedied when the slump in the cotton industry brought some much needed labour through the shed doors and engines began to look more presentable. At Lees, though, this influx of labour created something of a problem because there was not that much work to keep the newcomers busy; all sorts of schemes were tried out including having the cleaners paint the background of smokebox numberplates, blue and red being the favourite colours. That practice was stopped when an inspector at Stockport Edgeley spotted a Lees engine at the station and did not take too kindly to the results. A similar pre–war innovation treated shedplates to a yellow background. Such was the individualism of the staff at Lees, due no doubt to them being out–on–a–limb so to speak, that many characters were born from its men (women only ever worked there as cleaners during the wars); there was one driver who had two sets of overalls with him whenever on duty, a 'street set and an oiling set'. Another gentleman who worked the Motor Link liked to keep his engine well oiled, so much so that he would hide oil bottles in all kinds of places 'just in case of a shortage'. Long after his retirement bottles were being found at Delph and Greenfield stations, all over Lees shed and even in the void under the bunker of a Class 3 tank. There was a man whose wife would be waiting at the office door every pay day so that she could relieve him of his hard earned wages, apparently if she didn't a local hostelry would have his company until closing time. Then there was 'Cannonball' who would do any job and go anywhere on anyday and drive any engine to boot even if he was not too familiar with its controls. He it was who once drove a ten coach excursion back from Blackpool to Stalybridge with a Standard 9F 2–10–0, the last bit of the journey from Manchester Victoria to Stalybridge and that includes Miles Platting bank, performed inadvertently with the tender brake on! He was heard to comment afterwards (with ample reason) 'the 9s would pull anything'.

J. Davenport.

84014 arrived at Lees in November 1955 in company with 84013 and 84019. Three other members of the class 84010, 84012 and 84015 had joined the complement in the previous year and were an immediate hit with the footplate crews. Although motor–fitted, they came too late to have any impact on the Delph workings, the reason for their arrival anyway; but they were put to good use during their stay. All six had gone by May 1959, divided between Bolton and Rose Grove (Burnley) sheds. This midday view in the early spring of 1956 shows the newly constructed shed roof and a yard covered in snow from an overnight fall.

J. Davenport.

A distinguished visitor in disgrace. Edge Hill based Patriot No.45538 *GIGGLESWICK* languishes on Lees after failing at Stalybridge whilst hauling a Manchester Exchange – Leeds semi–fast in 1956. A boiler water gauge gave a false reading and the resultant lack of water damaged the firebox crown requiring a visit to main works. Within 48 hours the Patriot was hauled to Crewe for repair.

J. Davenport.

The Fowler 7F 0–8–0, an enlarged but less successful version of the Midland Railway 4F 0–6–0. The coming of the Austerity 2–8–0s saw the demise of these engines not just from Lees but from the London Midland Region.

J. Davenport.

Over the years Lees had seen many types of engines temporarily transferred onto its allocation books, some for weeks, others staying longer. LMS 4F 0–6–0s and 8F 2–8–0s were amongst those tried in the post war period but visiting engines from sheds such as Gorton, Longsight, Newton Heath, Patricroft and further afield brought a variety that was sometimes lacking at Lees. It wasn't unknown for Lees to hold on to a particular 'good un' for as long as possible, a practice frowned upon in higher echelons but carried out nearly everywhere whenever the opportunity arose. This Longsight 4F was on regular rostered work, standing in for the usual Stanier 8F 2–8–0, and had worked in on the 5.20 a.m. Stockport Edgeley – Oldham Glodwick Road freight. It was ultimately employed on the 10.22 a.m. Diggle – Mold Junction the following day after a trip into Yorkshire.

J. Davenport.

90589 was another of Lees WD 2–8–0s, showing, for those interested, many minor detail differences from 90525. Formerly a Wester Region engine, 90589 had been well and truly 'Swindonised' with Swindon lamp brackets and boiler fittings; non–WR sheds having the misfortune to have one of these ex–WR Austerities had to stock additional spares. Having just come on shed, 90589 stands between the shed and the old coaling stage waiting to have its fire cleaned and tender replenished. The last locomotive to exit Lees shed was a WD, No.90708. The event happened at 10.15 p.m. on Saturday 11th April 1964. The shift foreman, who had booked on duty just 15 minutes previously, described that shift as one of the loneliest nights he had ever spent in his life; the shed being empty from the time that the WD and its crew left to work the Ashton Moss Trips. Official closure occured on the following Monday.

A Farnley Junction, Leeds, 'Crab' No.42713 passes Lees in June 1955 with a Clegg Street – Scarborough relief. In the warehouse opposite withdrawn engines would be stored at various times.

J. Davenport.

Ex–L&Y Class 2P 2–4–2T No.50731 of Bolton shed arrives at Lees station on a Delph – Oldham Clegg Street motor train in April 1953. The temporary shortage of V.C.R. fitted Fowler Class 3 2–6–2Ts at Lees, due to their engines being in shops, forced them to borrow this foreigner.

J. Davenport.

A very derelict Lees station in June 1963 with the line to Oldham still in business, though not for much longer. The solid architecture of the buildings stands out well in the sunlight and no doubt could have made a substantial and attractive private residence.

M. J. Stretton.

GROTTON.

BR Standard 2MT 2–6–2 tank No. 84010 approaches Grotton with the 12.10 p.m. Delph *Donkey* from Clegg St in spring 1955. The train is made up of trailer coach M 3407 and motor coach M15846.

A. J. Cocker.

42115 starts away from Grotton & Springhead with its train for Stockport. The station building at this place is still intact, finding further use as a private residence; even some of the platform exists but all other remnants of the railway have disappeared. Lydgate tunnel, just visible behind the porter on the platform, was the longest in the Oldham area at 1,332 yards long and although the mouth at the east end can hardly be seen through overgrown vegetation, that at the Grotton end is still visible although bricked up. The tops of the ventilating shafts that once adorned the hill along the course of the tunnel have also gone, demolished, their brickwork pushed down the shafts into the void and the resulting hole sealed up.

A. J. Cocker.

Class '2' 2–6–0 No. 46452 stops at the closed Grotton & Springhead station whilst hauling the last goods train, for Greenfield and Mossley, out of Oldham over the old LNWR route on the 10th April 1964. The stop, for photographic purposes, was made to enable a small group of enthusiasts from the Locomotive Club of Great Britian, riding in a 'special' brakevan attached to the trains own brake at the rear of the train, to record the journey and the line itself. The following day it was to close completely, severing the rail link to Greenfield after 108 years. The station at Grotton had closed in April 1955 when services to Delph were curtailed and Lees shed lost its last regular passenger work.

I. G. Holt.

One of Lees' Fairburn 4MT 2–6–4 tanks No. 42115 emerges from Lydgate tunnel with the 12.27 p.m. Greenfield – Stockport stopping train, on the 30th April 1955.

J. Davenport.

After performing its duties at Mossley and Greenfield No. 46452 returned to Oldham propelling the two brakevans with the 'special' at the front. Stops were made at various places for the benefit of the enthusiasts who were also lucky enough to be blessed with some spring sunshine. In the deep cutting at the east end of Lydgate tunnel the train stops just beyond the site of Grasscroft Halt under the Mossley Road bridge. Today this cutting is filled with a rich vegetation of trees and bushes and even from the vantage point of the road bridge it is difficult to distinguish the tunnel portal.

I. G. Holt.

ROYTON JUNCTION.

Newton Heath 'Crabs' figured prominently in the 'Wakes specials' motive power pool and No.42703 returns the empty stock of a Rhyl – Oldham working to Lightbowne carriage sidings Manchester, via Rochdale, on the last day of June 1956. To the left, a Lanky A Class shunts loaded coal wagons into Royton Junction Up yard.

P. Hutchinson.

The Higginshaw group of Down sidings at Royton Junction from Yates Street bridge on a wet Thursday, just prior to Wakes, in June 1958. Coaching stock is positioned ready for the following evening when the train nearest the camera will form a service to the West Country. Loaded coal wagons along with empty tar tanks await entry into Higginshaw gas works. A scrap yard fills this site today and the cotton mills in the background, *Holyrood* and *Tay*, are long gone, the former destroyed by a spectacular fire in December 1961.

Oldham Evening Chronicle.

This unusual signal, captured on film in May 1961, was sited in Derker Street where, until a few years previously, it controlled road traffic whenever a train was passing over the tracks (no longer in situ) that linked Messrs Platts Old Hartford works with the Hartford goods yard. Like the yard, the signal is long gone but some of the track formerly serving the Platts works is still visible in nearby Gould Street.

R. S. Greenwood.

Having disgorged its returning holidaymakers at Mumps, another empty stock train threads Royton Junction en route for Manchester behind 2P 4–4–0 No.40680 and an unidentified Stanier Class 5. Just above the engines, behind the first range of buildings and at an angle to the line, stands the former L&Y cotton warehouse in Hartford goods yard. July 1957.
J. Davenport.

Higginshaw sidings from Holyrood Street bridge on the evening of 6th June 1967 with a Newton Heath Stanier 8F 2–8–0, No.48758, remarshalling its train, the Oldham Mumps – Moston 'pick–up'. Yates Street bridge is, like its surroundings, in a somewhat dilapidated state compared with views from the 1950s. It is interesting to see the main running lines receiving attention, with new ballast in place as it was a decade earlier. Later developments saw the running lines slewed to the left with the kink taken out and a timber built halt, fittingly named Derker and replacing the closed and virtually isolated station at Royton Junction, erected at a more convenient location just by the bridge. Renamed Royton, Royton Junction was still open (for two trains a day) some months after Derker opened and until closure procedures were completed.

P. Hutchinson.

Overall view of the junction in June 1955 with Class 5 4–6–0 No.44696 passing through with empty stock from Lightbowne carriage sidings to Mumps to form a 2.30 p.m. Wakes excursion to Blackpool.

J. Davenport.

Stanier Class 4 tank No.42550 works a Rochdale – Manchester train bunker first out of Royton Junction on the 18th June 1955. The five coach train was typical of the period and its makeup of both suburban and corridor stock could also be described as not unusual. The lack of activity in the adjacent yard signifies that this is a Saturday afternoon.

P. Hutchinson.

Ex–L&Y Aspinall 0–6–0 saddletanks, rebuilt from Barton Wright tender engines, were favourites for the Royton Junction pilot job and No.51371 goes about its business in April 1960, en route to Higginshaw gas works to pick up some full tar tanks. On the left is a reminder of Oldham's past with tens of thousands of cotton bobbins tipped on the site of the derelict *Tay* mill.

P. Hutchinson.

A Lees 'A' Class does a spell of afternoon sorting in the Up yard during July 1956. To the right of the parachute water tank is Fowler G3 0–8–0 No.49667, one of a type which was then nearing the end of its working life having had a somewhat disappointing career spending more time as liabilities than assets.

J. Davenport.

A Nuneaton based G2 0–8–0, No.49142, glides through the junction, in May 1957, ready to back down to the yard to pick up its train. Although plentiful at one time in the Oldham area (Lees housed at least half a dozen until the end of the 1930s) these ex–LNW engines were not too common from the mid 1950s, although a daily goods train from Stockport to Glodwick Road yard sometimes brought an Edgeley G2 over the OA&GB. In the yard WD 2–8–0 No.90671, from Lees shed, sorts a train of empty wagons.

J. Davenport.

The highest point on the old L&Y Oldham branch, Royton Junction, stands 613 feet above sea level. Royton itself, just over a mile distant, was some 85 feet lower, the branch boasting an incline of 1 in 62 for much of its length making doubleheading of heavy excursion trains out of the town to the junction a necessity more often than not. Largest of the goods yards in the area, Royton Junction was mainly sorting sidings dealing with trains coming into Oldham from near and far to be rearranged ready for distribution to local industry and goods yards. In latter years its tracks were filled with stored wagons of all types. It was, according to one former driver, not the place to be on a cold windy day. Royton Junction signalbox was one of three to be found in the area of the yards, it was sited alongside the junction proper controlling traffic from the branch as well as through traffic from the Oldham and Rochdale directions. A few hundred yards to the north was Royton Junction Siding box, dating from 1893, which on the morning of Wednesday May 1st 1963 was virtually demolished by a runaway loaded coal wagon; an accident that sealed its fate as it was never rebuilt. Royton Junction signalbox was erected in the 1880s and after major alterations and additions to the track layout at the junction in the early years of the century it ended up with 38 working levers and 4 spare. 28th March 1966.

R. S. Greenwood.

Another Stanier 2–6–4T, this time unlined No.42621, brings an afternoon train off the Royton branch bound for Manchester Victoria on the same day. Newton Heath shed, with Agecroft participating, provided the bulk of the locomotives for the Oldham area suburban services over the ex–L&Y lines, former LMS 2–6–4Ts being ideal for the job; other 2–6–4Ts noted on local services this day included 42180, 42283, 42286, 42486, 42645 and BR Standard 80087. Other engine sheds supplying motive power during weekdays included Bank Hall, Blackpool, Bury and Wigan Central. To the left of the telegraph pole, alongside the station platforms, can be seen the 'continuous pilot' coal stage where for upwards of sixty years Newton Heath tank engines, with the occasional tender engine performing, replenished bunker coal stocks during a six day stint shunting the yards around the clock.

J. Davenport.

Patricroft based G2, No.49199, takes on water from the parachute tank alongside No.2 goods loop, behind Royton Junction station, after arrival with the 8.00 a.m. Mondays only freight from Patricroft in early May 1961. The footpath linking the station with Holyrood Street was a good vantage point for observing trains in close proximity. In the latter years of the 1950s and the early 60s, goods wagons requiring repair were sent to Royton Junction yard from all over the London Midland Region to be inspected by a team of men who classified the wagons as either fit for repair or scrap.

R. S. Greenwood.

WD No.90589 sets out from the Royton Junction No.2 Up Goods loop with a short coal train, bound for Oldham, in April 1960. Above the engine the Royton branch can be seen heading off to the west, a 15 miles per hour speed limit sign warns of the severity of the curvature through the station.

P. Hutchinson.

Although usually a Newton Heath 9F 2–10–0 turn, the daily Carlisle – Oldham Glodwick Road empty van train could often be counted on, by enthusiasts, to produce one of the rarer Stanier Class 5s. Either a Carlisle Kingmoor or Scottish area engine would be in charge then and the motive power on the 26th June 1965 was no exception with 45112 of Kingmoor shed easing its long load over the last mile of its journey.

P. Hutchinson.

DOWN TO ROYTON.

Stanier Class 4MT 2–6–4T 42651 coasts down the 1 in 62 gradient, near Turf Lane bridge, towards Royton with a train from Manchester Victoria in 1958.

J. Davenport.

Royton terminus, summer 1960. The single platform terminus was opened on the 21st March 1864. Served by a single track branch line at first, Royton had quite an extensive goods yard complete with the inevitable cotton warehouse/goods shed. Redundant coaching stock of all descriptions are positioned for their impending scrap. Many old vehicles including sleeping cars but especially suburban stock were brought to Royton for breaking up during the late 1950s and early 60s. In actual fact only the coach bodies were scrapped, the underframes and bogies retained for conversion into 'Carflats', for both passenger Motorail traffic and 'Company trains'. Lees shed provided an Austerity 2–8–0 as pilot at Royton such was the weight of the scrapping traffic and inevitably remnants of the coach interiors — mirrors, carpets from 1st Class and even chicken wire from the asbestos insulation found its way back to Lees, its front rooms and pigeon lofts.

Oldham Evening Chronicle.

Royton Station signalbox in 1965. Completely timber built, the box dating from 1908 contained 53 working levers and was the largest in the Oldham area. Replacing an earlier structure, it was erected during a large scale resignalling of the Royton terminus in 1907/08 during which time the Board of Trade tried to persuade the L&Y to provide a second platform. The Board's first comments on the 13th Feb 1907 run... *this is a case in which a short branch double line only a mile or so in length ends in a single platform line but from my knowledge of the place I know it would be difficult to get a second platform and the new works proposals are only an extension of the goods yard consequent upon the great increase in traffic. The company's attention might be drawn to the point and asked if they cannot see their way to double the line and add a second platform. If they cannot do so this provisional sanction may I consider be given....* The Lancashire and Yorkshire reply 14th March 1907 *...as to the remarks as to a short double line terminating in a single platform, I beg to inform you that my directors have now considered the suggestions of the BOT and they desire me to state that very considerable difficulty and expense would be involved in providing a second platform at this station as will be explained to your officer on the occasion of his inspection of the alterations. The line is only a short branch one and there are facing points on the down main line which can be set for the protection of trains standing in the platform...* The L&Y reported 30th June 1908... *that the works are now completed and ready for inspection...* Col Druitt inspected in August 1908... *at this place a large number of additional sidings have been provided and the connections entirely re-arranged. A new signal box has been erected in place of an old one, containing 53 working and 7 spare levers and the place has been practically resignalled throughout. The interlocking and other arrangements being satisfactory I can recommend etc...*

R. S. Greenwood.

Two Stanier Class 5s, Nos.45114 and 45101, prepare to leave Royton with an excursion for Southport in April 1965. The leading engine would assist as far as Mumps from where the running would be mostly downhill but before that some stiff gradients would be encountered on the way to Royton Jct; the first 4 chains at 1 in 150 followed by 14 chains of 1 in 71 then the taxing 67 chains of 1 in 62, this then levelling off for the run through the Junction station. 45114 was a visitor from Aston shed in Birmingham.

I. G. Holt.

The introduction of diesel multiple units onto the Royton branch was brought home with a vengeance to local residents one cold and damp February morning in 1961 when a runaway unit, coming down the branch to form the first of the days' services to Manchester, crashed through the buffer stops, crossed over Highbarn Street and continued on through a pair of terraced houses giving the tenants a somewhat alarming if not horrific early morning call. Rescuers were soon on the scene and miraculously found everyone involved to be alive, the only serious injury was to the driver who had jumped as the train went through the platform. This view of the scene, taken later that same morning, shows the extent of damage to the property, which had to be demolished once the unit was extricated.

R. S. Greenwood.

Closed 16th April 1966, Royton's station was doomed because it was not on the *main line*. Passenger traffic could not support the cost of keeping the branch in place and much of the goods that once transited through the depot was either lost to road or did not exist anymore. The tracks of the branch were taken up shortly after closure and the station demolished; much of the track in the goods yard had been lifted some months earlier. This August 1964 view with a Derby built two car dmu waiting at the single platform shows much detail that no longer exists – gas lights adorn the stone wall which had been recently cut down to less than half its original height. The engine run–round line, so essential in terminal stations, looks has though it hasn't seen much use in years. Timber built coal merchants offices line the rear of the mineral yard, diminutive alongside the railway's weigh office. To the left and still in use is the huge warehouse built on the same scale as the cotton mills it was built to serve. Rumour has it that a ghost once stalked its cellar. Perhaps the ghost was laid to rest when the building was demolished.

J. J. Smith.

Royton goods yard *circa* 1920. Two Lancashire & Yorkshire Railway official photographs taken to show off one of the latest Company innovations of the time – palletisation. As far as the author is aware nothing came of this method of transfer in the 1920s but in recent times the idea has become widely used. The quality of the views show some interesting peripheral detail.

National Railway Museum.

Fowler Class 4 2–6–4T 42343, a type used extensively on passenger trains in the area during the 1930s and 40s, about to run round the LCGB North West Branch Brake Van tour at Royton station, on the 7th August 1965.

I. G. Holt.

Southport was just one of the Lancashire coast resorts ideally situated for a day away from the drab surrounding of the cotton towns. Every year tens of thousands would journey on day or weekend trips to the seaside at Easter mostly by train and on Easter Saturday 1960 Ivatt Class 4 No. 42288 piloted by Stanier Class 5 No. 44845, running tender first, haul a loaded excursion full of day–trippers out of Royton and off to the beaches.

P. Hutchinson.

Higginshaw Gas Works required about six hundred tons of coal a day in order to maintain the eight million cubic feet of town gas supplied to the area. Most of that coal came by rail with small train loads brought from Royton Jct sidings at various periods during the day. A rather steep incline had to be negotiated in order to gain access to the gas works hence the small train loads. The Royton Junction pilot was responsible for making the short (just over ¼ mile) trips and once it had surmounted the incline, handing over its train to one of the gas works own shunting engines it would return with a rake of empties. Two small engine sheds housed the Higginshaw Gas Works stud which in 1952 consisted of three ancient though reliable Peckett tanks and an Avonside tank of more recent vintage:- *HIGGINSHAW* 0–6–0 outside cylinder saddle tank built by Peckett & Sons Ltd. No. 460 of 1887. *CASTLESHAW* 0–6–0 inside cylinder saddle tank built by Peckett & Sons Ltd. No. 465 of 1887. *MAYORESS* 0–4–0 outside cylinder saddle tank built by Peckett & Sons Ltd. No. 1023 of 1905. *POLLARD* 0–4–0 outside cylinder saddle tank built by Avonside Engine Co. No. 1912 of 1922. This Sunday morning view from Higginshaw Lane roadbridge in the summer of 1958 shows the incline climbing sharply away from the Royton branch to gain access to the gas works site. WD Austerity 2–8–0s Nos. 90271 and 90708 help out with the relaying of the Royton branch.

J. Davenport.

As late as October 1966 steam locomotives still worked the Royton Junction pilot turn and condenser–gear fitted Jinty No. 47202, a latecomer to the area and minus front numberplate, arrives at the top of the gas works incline to collect a train of empties. Just behind the rear lamp of the brakevan can be seen the Higginshaw sidings signalbox, manned throughout the day Monday to Friday and mornings only on Saturdays, a somewhat extended period compared to wartime manning (see table).

R. S. Greenwood.

Typical of many private concerns, the Gas Department of Oldham Corporation maintained its own fleet of wagons to carry coal from the various collieries to the gas works at Higginshaw and the smaller plant near Rhodes Bank. These photographs, taken at the builders works at Horbury near Wakefield, show two such wagons ordered in May 1936 from Charles Roberts & Co. Ltd. Five of the traditional wooden types were delivered and, apparently for evaluation purposes, two of the all–steel bodied examples were purchased. Both types were of 12 tons capacity and sported the Gas Department red oxide livery with white letters shaded black.

courtesy W. Hudson.

ONTO SHAW & CROMPTON.

October 1960 found an extremely rare visitor to the Oldham – Rochdale line, ex–LNER Gresley K3 2–6–0 No.61965, at the head of a Royton Junction – Moston Saturday freight, at Heyside between the Junction and Shaw. When ones sees photographs of loaded freight trains such as these it becomes difficult to understand why there is such a small amount of like traffic on the modern system of today.

R. S. Greenwood.

A superb study of Lancashire & Yorkshire architecture at Shaw & Crompton in October 1958. The timber built signalbox on the left dates from about the mid 1880s; it was supplied and erected by the Railway Signal Company Ltd. Designated a Size 4 by the L&Y, it was called simply Shaw South (later Shaw Station), there being another box on the opposite side of the line near to Linney Lane bridge called Shaw North. The level crossing gates were introduced at about the same time as the signalbox became operational, prior to this Beal Lane was ungated and a crossing keeper was employed to control the road traffic whenever a train passed over the crossing. The keepers cottage, a tiny two storey building, was situated opposite the South signalbox alongside the Briar mill entrance. This cottage was apparently the first Shaw signalbox. Also coinciding with the introduction of the crossing gates was this footbridge No.39, necessary to allow pedestrians to cross over the railway when the gates were closed. Still in its original condition, the bridge was to be renewed in the early 1960s with a precast concrete walkway replacing the wooden structure but utilising the stone piers. The station buildings were also of stone construction, with the locally found variety put to use. The Up side platform buildings originally consisted of a single waiting shed, but in 1897 a glass and timber frontage was added and a general waiting room was created with a divide forming a ladies waiting room alongside. A canopy never graced this platform. The structures on the Down platform remain pretty much as they were built for the opening of the line. Today two pathetic bus shelter affairs serve as covered waiting accommodation. The attractive lattice footbridge became another victim of BR rationalisation at Shaw, connecting the two platforms it was a late addition to the station being erected in 1888 and costing £120. To finish this late 1950s scene, one of the then newly introduced Cravens twin–car diesel multiple units coasts into the station bound for Oldham and Manchester.

Authors collection.

Fowler 4F 0–6–0 No.44543 leaving Shaw with the 6.0 p.m. Manchester to Rochdale via Oldham train on Friday the 4th July 1958. Suprisingly the three cotton mills in the picture, *Lily No. 1, Lilac* and *Briar* are all still standing albeit in use for other purposes and are employing a good number of local workers in what might be described as service industry jobs. To the left of the passenger train is another once regular sight that is no longer with us, the tractor train loaded with new vehicles built in the Coventry area and bound for storage in empty cotton mills, awaiting shipment from Liverpool. About once a week the tractor train would usually arrive behind a Nuneaton based G2. To the right is the huge five storey goods shed–cum–cotton warehouse built 1886/88 at a cost of £13,313, once a hive of activity receiving, storing and dispatching thousands of bales of raw cotton every year to the three dozen mills scattered around Shaw. The first warehouse, a single storey building, was erected for the opening of the line in 1863 with a four storey extension added in 1872. Extensions were made to the goods yard at various times, for instance during May to July 1884 additional sidings were laid costing just over £500. Linney Lane bridge was widened during 1893–4, at a cost of £3,177, to accommodate further sidings and a headshunt. The goods yard was equipped with a 5 ton timber jibbed crane, complemented by another of 3 tons capacity and a small 15 cwt lorry crane. Inside the warehouses nine gas powered friction jiggers of 8 and 16 cwt capacities were installed. Just above the third coach of the train was the one time spur leading off to a colliery at Bankhouse on Grains Road. Although these local collieries existed (there were five in 1830), they could never produce enough coal for the hungry mills of Shaw and its townspeople, so trainloads were brought daily from both the Yorkshire and Lancashire fields to satisfy demand.

P. Hutchinson.

L&YR cast iron gradient post, Down side, Shaw, February 1961.

R. S. Greenwood.

Old meets new at Shaw in June 1964. Britannia Pacific No.70045 *LORD ROWALLAN*, on a weekend Shaw – Blackpool extra, pulls over Beal Lane crossing with a train of non–corridor stock whilst a Derby Lightweight DMU approaches on a Rochdale service. Notice the new pre–cast bridge walkway.

I. G. Holt.

A long train of 16 ton mineral wagons loaded with Yorkshire coal and bound for Higginshaw gas works pulls through the curve between Dunwood Park and Railway View, Shaw, in early June 1966, behind Heaton Mersey 8F 2–8–0 No. 48684. The view, from Bridge Street footbridge, has changed somewhat today, the lineside hut and the bridge spanning the rear of the train have both gone and the line itself is singled, the track nearest the camera was lifted in 1980, after the whole route between Shaw and Rochdale was singled on July 6th of that year. Goods trains are also history now except for the very rare diversion from the Calder Valley line.

R. S. Greenwood.

Jubilee, Shaw circa 1905. Dominated by the colliery, this the narrowest part of the valley formed by the river Beal, has been a road traffic blackspot for many years simply because of the bridge built for the opening of the railway in 1863. With the coming of the line drastic changes took place as regards the road, which had to be realigned to make space for the course of the railway. Apparently the original Jubilee public house was in the path of the railway and had to be demolished, the present establishment being a new building erected at the expense of the Lancashire & Yorkshire Railway. Certainly there was a range of buildings on Tithe's 1849 map which were big enough to have been a public house and would have been in the way of the alignment of the railway. The Jubilee Colliery (owned by the Oldham, Middleton & Rochdale Coal Co. Ltd until 1883) was one of three (the others were Butterworth Colliery at Milnrow and Moston Colliery at Moston) owned by Platt Brothers, once Oldham's largest employer with a workforce at one time of over 12,000. Producing thousands of tons of coal a year Jubilee had, as can be seen, its own sidings complete with loading chutes for tipping the coal into the wagons of the company's fleet. However, the bulk of the coal mined at Jubilee was converted into coke on site in the two large ovens, part of which can be seen on the left. The coke operation here and at the nearby Butterworth Hall colliery in Milnrow produced enough fuel to feed the company's numerous forges at the Oldham works, what little coal was surplus fed the boilers. It is not known if Platt Bros. ever employed a locomotive at Jubilee, more likely than not a horse would be used to manoeuvre wagons about the place, but the compact system could at sometime have used a single locomotive due to the traffic and tonnages involved in making up a train load for dispatch to the main works in Oldham. Perhaps the L&Y locomotive did the shunting when it returned empties and picked up full wagonloads. The L&Y Working Timetable Appendix of 1921 states that.... *Wagons for Jubilee siding are to be worked there by a pilot engine from either Shaw or Milnrow.....* There was from 1889 a signalbox opposite the colliery sidings which was still operational in the 1930s but by 1940 it had been abandoned no doubt at the same time as the mining operation. Modellers might like to know that Platts wagons were painted blue, with white lettering, for mineral wagons and red oxide, with white lettering, for goods wagons.

Jubilee, Shaw.